Textiles

and Technology

(UK edition)

Adapted by Margaret Beith

from the book by

stine Oppermann and Kate Baulch

CAMBRIDGE
UNIVERSITY PRESS

PUBLISHED BY THE PRESS SYNDICATE OF THE UNIVERSITY OF CAMBRIDGE
The Pitt Building, Trumpington Street, Cambridge CB2 1RP, United Kingdom

CAMBRIDGE UNIVERSITY PRESS
The Edinburgh Building, Cambridge CB2 2RU, United Kingdom
40 West 20th Street, New York, NY 10011–4211, USA
10 Stamford Road, Oakleigh, Melbourne 3166, Australia

© Cambridge University Press 1997

First published 1997

Printed in Great Britain at the University Press, Cambridge

A catalogue record for this book is available from the British Library

ISBN 0 521 57657 1 (paperback)

Notice to teachers

It is illegal to reproduce any part of this work in material form
(including photocopying and electronic storage) except under
the following circumstances:
(i) where you are abiding by a licence granted to your school or institution
by the Copyright Licensing Agency;
(ii) where no such licence exists, or where you wish to exceed the terms of
a licence, and you have gained the written permission of Cambridge
University Press;
(iii) where you are allowed to reproduce without permission under the
provisions of Chapter 3 of the Copyright, Designs and Patents Act 1988.

Acknowledgements

The authors and publisher would like to thank MODUS/
Dr S K Mukhopadhyay for permission to reproduce the table on page 94.

The authors and publishers would like to thank the following for
permission to reproduce copyright photographs.

A–Z Botanical Collection 4tr;
Art Directors Photo Library 14;
Margaret Beith 3bl;
Eur. Ing. Richard Beith 18, 77, 79, 80, 81;
Cape Insulation Products Limited 6;
Emmerich (Berlon) Ltd. 88tr;
Mary Evans Picture Library 87, 89tl;
Luke Eyres 89br;
Paul Franklin/Oxford Scientific Films 13;
Lizzie Keiss 5br;
Andrew Lambert 4bl, 4br, 5tr, 8, 19br, 70;
Laura Ashley 85;
Nuno Corporation 29br;
Graham Portlock 3tr, 16, 17, 23, 24, 25, 27, 37, 53, 54, 55tr, 60, 67, 85,
89tr, 89bl, 89br;
Lizzie Reakes 93;
Scientific American 89tl;
David Toase 29tl;
Warrington Fire research Limited 31;
Borias Machine Company Ltd. 88tl;
Grodania A/S Wern Tarw 92.

Contents

1 Introduction to textiles — 1

What are textiles? — 1
Setting up a database — 3
Natural fibres — 4
Synthetic fibres — 7

2 From fibre to fabric — 10

Fibre processing — 10
Woven fabrics — 14
Knitted fabrics — 17
Other fabrics — 18
Carpet weaving — 18
Lace making — 19
Leather — 19
Extending your database — 19

3 Enhancement of fabrics — 21

Combining fabrics — 21
Adding colour to fabrics — 22
Surface decoration techniques — 25
Surface finishes — 28

4 Choosing fabrics for a purpose — 31

The properties of fabrics — 31
British Standards for textiles — 36
Labelling and consumer rights legislation relating to textiles — 36
Care and maintenance of textiles products — 37

5 Influences on the design and manufacture of textile products — 39

How to research — 39
The factors involved in consumer choice — 44

6 How textile products are made 46

Disassembling	46
Tools and equipment	46
Basic construction techniques	49
Fastenings	53
Computer-aided manufacture (CAM)	55

7 Design 57

Basic design principles	58
Ergonomics	61
Aesthetics	61
Recognising a need for design	62
The design brief	64
Drawing up a specification	66
Planning your project	66
Generating design solutions	67
Presenting design solutions	68
Developing the design for making	69

8 Production of textile items 72

Systems	72
The importance of good organisation and systematic working in the manufacture of textile goods	74
Types of production systems	75
Case studies	75

9 Selling 82

Advertising	82
Packaging	83
Displaying goods	85

10 Back to the future 87

Influences of technology on the textile industry in the past	87
Influences of changes in technology on textile products	90
Environmental issues relating to textiles	93
Uses of technical textiles	94

Glossary 97

Index 99

1 Introduction to textiles

There have been technological changes in the area of textiles from earliest times. For thousands of years people have been clothing themselves for protection, adornment and decoration, first with animal skins, later with twisted and interlaced leaves and stems of plants. When people settled to cultivate the land, they were able to produce good-quality fibres from plants and animals. The synthetic fibres developed in the twentieth century have produced a wide range of textiles and textile products with many domestic and industrial uses.

This chapter focuses on:

> what textiles are,

> setting up a database for your work in textiles,

> the origins and basic composition of natural fibres such as cotton, wool, cashmere and silk,

> the origins and basic composition of synthetic fibres such as nylon, polyester and viscose.

What are textiles?

The word 'textile' comes from the Latin word *texere*, which means 'to weave'. Theoretically, textile still means this. However, it is now applied in much broader terms to all **fibres**, yarns and other materials that are made into fabrics.

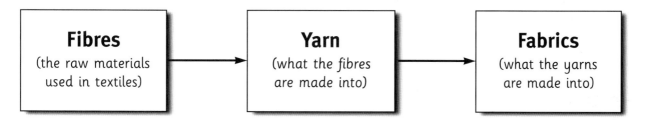

| **Fibres** (the raw materials used in textiles) | → | **Yarn** (what the fibres are made into) | → | **Fabrics** (what the yarns are made into) |

Flowchart: from fibre to fabric.

You will come into contact with products made from textiles every day. Although clothing is perhaps the most widely recognised form of textiles today, textiles are also evident in many other places:

> in the home – as furnishings, curtains, cushions, carpets,

> in industry – as ropes, tarpaulin covers, and linings,

> in leisure goods – as sails for boats, balloons, ropes, backpacks.

Uses for textiles.

Parachute

Tarpaulin

Carpet

Curtains

Seat covering

Setting up a database

There are so many different fibres that you cannot be expected to know everything about them all. However, you can set up a relational database of information about the various fibres. This is a set of records which is organised so that you can make comparisons.

You could use a card index and organise the information for each item so that qualities can be easily compared.

> *Advantage* – samples of the materials can be attached to the cards.

> *Disadvantage* – sorting through cards can be very slow.

You can also use a computer. Database programs are really electronic card indexes where the cards appear as pictures on a computer screen. The database is able to sort through the records very quickly for fabrics with the qualities that you want. You need to think carefully about how to structure your database before you begin. You need to know about one fibre from each of the main groups:

> natural
> – plant
> – animal
> – mineral

> synthetic
> – cellulosic
> – non-cellulosic.

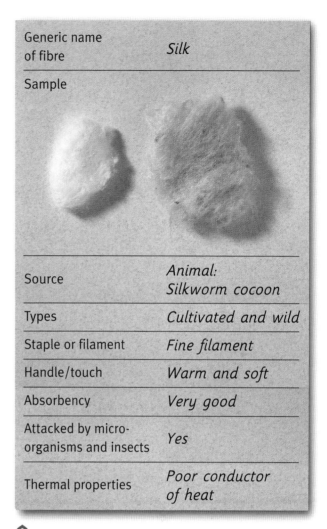

Generic name of fibre	*Silk*
Sample	
Source	*Animal: Silkworm cocoon*
Types	*Cultivated and wild*
Staple or filament	*Fine filament*
Handle/touch	*Warm and soft*
Absorbency	*Very good*
Attacked by micro-organisms and insects	*Yes*
Thermal properties	*Poor conductor of heat*

Database card.

It takes time to collect the information and build your database, so you should begin as soon as you have worked out the structure and add information as you proceed through the course. Decide how much time you can afford to spend on building your database and try to keep to your timetable. If you spend too little time, you will find it difficult later; if you spend too much time you may be doing unnecessary work.

‹ A screen from a database.

Natural fibres

Natural fibres come from three sources: plants, animals and minerals.

Plant fibres

Plant fibres are made of woody substances which include **cellulose** and are therefore referred to as cellulosic fibres. Some of the fibres are part of the transport system that carries water, minerals and waste products around the plant. If you look at plant fibres under a microscope you will see that they are tubes. Some of them will be flattened and broken but many will be undamaged. Water can get into the fibres because they are tubular. This means that plant fibres produce the most absorbent fabrics. The best-known are flax (which is used to make linen) and cotton.

Flax

Flax is a small plant with blue flowers. The leaves and stalks of the flax plant are made into linen, which is a strong and cool material used for making clothing, tablecloths, napkins and laces. Flax was the first plant to be grown for spinning and weaving, and probably the first to be used for making textiles (traces of it have been found from over 4000 years ago). To make linen, the plant needs to be pulled from the ground as some of the most valuable parts of the plant are in the lower stem and roots. The stalks with roots attached are soaked in water until the green part rots away. This process is called **retting**. The fibres that are left after retting can be separated and dried. Once dry, they are scraped to remove any dirt, and combed to leave the fibres straight and parallel to one another – ready to be spun and woven into linen. The seeds are harvested to make linseed oil.

Close-up of a single flax plant.

Cotton

Cotton is the most widely used textile fibre. The cotton plant grows to about 1.2–1.5 m in height. After flowering, a pod or 'boll' about the size of a walnut remains on the flowering stalk. When it is ripe, the boll bursts open and forms a ball of cotton wool, called a **lint**. The lint is picked and the cotton in the lint is separated from the hairs by beating it with a stick. This process is called **ginning**. The raw cotton is then packed tightly in bales and sent to mills.

A close-up of a lint, showing rough side.

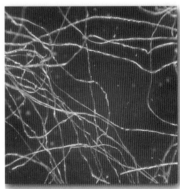

Cotton fibres under a microscope (x20).

Animal fibres

All animal fibres are made of protein and are therefore called **proteinic fibres**. The two best-known animal fibres are wool and silk.

Wool

Wool is the soft, warm, springy hair that grows on sheep. It grows in the same way as human hair. Small cells grow from the root of the hair and gradually die. If you look at wool under a microscope you will see that the fibres look scaly and crinkly.

Sheep are reared for both wool and meat. Some breeds are better for meat and some breeds are noted for the special quality of their wool.

The fleeces are usually removed from the sheep using electric shears. Hand shearing is used where there is no electricity supply. Fleeces can weigh from 1 to 7 kg. The fleeces can be sorted in four ways.

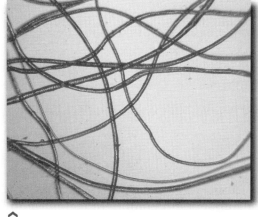

Wool fibres under a microscope (x40).

1 Whether it is suitable for worsted, woollen or felt processing. You will learn about these processes in Chapter 2.

2 The fineness or coarseness of the wool.

3 The grade as assessed by fibre length, colour or contamination.

4 The percentage of wool that is left after dirt, grease and undesirable fibres are removed.

The quality of the wool determines how it is used.

Sheep shearing.

Quality of wool	Uses	Breeds it comes from
Fine wool	Top-quality clothing	Merino, Ramboillet, Southdown, Hampshire
Medium wool	Garments and blankets	Cheviot, Columbia, Corriedale, Dorset, dark-faced British breeds
Long, coarser wool	Carpet production	Leicester, Romney, Swaledale

Cashmere

Cashmere is similar to wool and is made from the hair of the Kashmir goat. It is very much lighter and warmer than wool and is particularly useful for golfers' sweaters, for example, as they require warmth but do not want bulky clothing. The fibre is normally imported, but there is a growing interest in keeping herds of Kashmir goats in Britain.

Silk

Silk is produced by silkworms, which are the caterpillars of several species of moth. The most important species is the *Bombyx mori* which lives in mulberry trees. (It can live on other leaves, but it will not produce such a fine, continuous filament.) The silk comes from the caterpillar's cocoon. After hatching, silkworms feed for several weeks before spinning their cocoon.

A liquid is secreted through two tiny glands in the worm's head and forms two fine filaments which are gummed together into a delicate thread. The silkworm then winds the thread around itself until it is eventually fully enclosed. At this stage, under natural conditions, the silkworm would finish the process and turn into a moth. In silk farms, they are killed and dropped into hot water to loosen the gum and give access to the thread.

Silk is an expensive fabric because the process of obtaining the fibre and making it into thread is quite arduous. Silk is lustrous, shiny and strong. China produces more raw silk than any other country. In the early nineteenth century, Japan was the largest producer, but now concentrates on producing silk which is made into the highest-quality fabrics.

Mineral fibres

This small group of fibres has fairly limited uses. Silica fibres, mineral wool (glass wool and rock wool) and asbestos are important for their fireproof qualities. Asbestos occurs naturally and was used quite widely until it was found that the dust causes asbestosis and lung cancer. Mineral fibres are made by melting minerals at very high temperatures and blowing compressed air into a stream of the liquid mineral to form fibres. Silica fibre is used in the manufacture of fire blankets. It is normally produced by chemical treatment of glass fibre textiles.

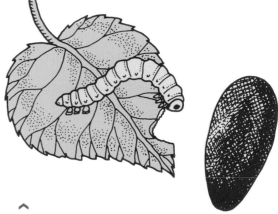

A silkworm feeding on a mulberry leaf, and its cocoon.

Silica fibre blankets can withstand very high temperatures.

Synthetic fibres

Synthetic fibres are made either partly or completely from chemicals and are divided into two categories:

> *cellulosic*   – fibres made from a natural base such as acetate, viscose, rayon and polyester,

> *non-cellulosic* – fibres made from a chemical base, such as nylon and acrylic.

Cellulosic fibres

Cellulose is a chemical found in plants. To make fibres for textiles, the cellulose is extracted and mixed with a number of chemicals. These chemicals vary, depending on the fibre to be made, but the end result is similar – a thick liquid which is then forced through the tiny holes of a **spinneret** to form threads. These threads are either hardened in acid and twisted into yarn or spun then twisted into yarn, depending on the type of fibre.

The first cellulosic fibre was **rayon**. In 1884, Count Hildaire de Chardonnet started to wonder what would happen if all the silkworms died. This led him to develop a replacement for silk. In 1889, he opened the first synthetic textiles factory. He called his fibre 'artificial silk' but it is better known today as **viscose**.

The fibres come from wood which is sawn into very fine pieces and mixed with water to form wood pulp. The pulp is soaked in caustic soda to untangle the extremely fine fibres. Carbon disulphide is added which changes the substance into solid yellow crumbs called xanthin. These 'crumbs' are soaked for several days in caustic soda. Provided the temperature and humidity are right, the fibres change into viscose. The viscose is then squirted into a bath of sulphuric acid, which changes it into pure cellulose fibres. The cellulose fibres can then be made into viscose yarn. Viscose has been used to make tassels, braids and sweaters.

Non-cellulosic fibres

These fibres are made from chemicals only. Tiny molecules, known as monomers, are joined into units which are in turn built into long chains called polymers. This process is called **polymerisation**. A liquid is formed by either heating or dissolving the chemicals, depending on the fibre being made. The liquid is forced through a spinneret and spun.

Nylon (which is a **polyamide**) was the first of this group of fibres. In the 1930s, scientists began to look for ways to make polymer fibres without using any wood or other natural substances. Two companies individually came up with a solution. In 1938, a team of scientists led by Dr Wallace Carothers at Du Pont Chemical Company in the USA came up with 'Fibre 6.6', later known as nylon. The Du Pont Company began to produce nylon commercially. In 1940, twelve years after the research began, it was used to make parachutes. Nylon stockings were sold to the public. These were the first nylon garments to be made commercially but workers in the factory were able to make their own garments from sub-standard 'parachute silk'.

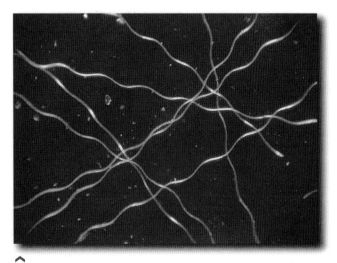

^
Nylon fibres under a microscope (x20).

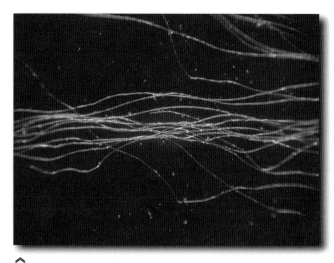

^
Polyester fibres under a microscope (x20).

In 1941, J. R. Quinfield and J. T. Dickson came up with a strong, synthetic fibre which could withstand very high temperatures. They called it **polyester**. The large European firm Imperial Chemical Industries (ICI) produced the fibre. Polyester has proved to be the most economically important synthetic fibre. Many new synthetic fibres have been developed, and are still being developed, from polyester. It is estimated that several new fibres reach world markets every week.

Summary

You should now be able to:

> describe what textiles are and where they are used,

> set up and use a database of information about fibres,

> describe the origin and basic composition of the natural fibres flax (linen), cotton, wool, cashmere, and silk,

> know some uses of mineral fibres,

> describe the origin and basic composition of the synthetic fibres rayon, viscose, nylon and polyester.

Activities

The information from these activities should be attractively presented and kept in your workfolder. This information will be useful to you as you progress through the course.

1 Choose a room in your house and list all the different types of textile that you can see there. Select five of these and explain their function.

2 Select three vehicles that you have seen on the road. Describe the function of the textiles used in their interior.

3 Take a small sample of any textile fabric and tease out some of the fibre. Try to identify the fibre. Stick your original sample and your fibre sample onto a sheet of paper and write some comments on the properties of the fibre and place it in your workfolder. You can add any other information and continue your investigations at any time.

4 Look at samples of fibre through the microscope. There should be a clear difference between the structure of plant and animal fibres. Make drawings of any samples which show the difference particularly well.

5 Fibres such as hemp and flax were selected for making textiles as a result of trying lots of different fibres. Nettle fibre has many of the qualities of flax. Why might a farmer prefer to grow flax?

6 Look for a plant which has strong fibres and try to reproduce the retting process described on page 4. Mount a sample of your fibre on a sheet of paper and describe its properties. Don't worry if your fibre does not have very much practical value; it is important that you make a sensible judgement about the materials that you reject.

7 Try to find out the length of filament that the silkworm spins to make a cocoon. You should find the information in the library or you could obtain some silk cocoons and estimate it for yourself. Cut a piece of card 100 mm wide and wind silk from a cocoon round the card, counting the number of turns. If you are interrupted, write the number on the card so that you don't forget it! Write down any observations that you make while doing this task.

Questions

1 Name one textile that comes from a plant and one that comes from an animal.

2 What is the name of the fibre made from flax?

3 What is the name of the most widely used natural fibre?

4 Wool is sorted in four ways. What are these?

5 What is the name of the fibre that comes from the Kashmir goat?

6 What is the correct name for artificial silk?

7 What is used to provide the fibres for making into rayon?

8 Why are mineral fibres important?

9 Name two fibres that are made from chemicals only.

10 Which company was the first to make polyester?

11 When was the first synthetic yarn produced?

12 What do silkworms eat? What happens if their diet is changed?

13 Why is flax uprooted rather than cut?

14 Why is cotton ginned after it is harvested?

2 From fibre to fabric

Fibres have to be processed before they can be made into fabrics.

This chapter focuses on:
> the various processes that fibres go through before they are made into fabrics,

> the construction of woven, knitted, and other fabrics.

Fibre processing

To make fabrics (other than felt and plastics) fibres need to be spun into yarn for weaving or knitting. The processes involved vary according to whether the fibre is a **staple** or a **filament**, the cleanliness of the fibre, and whether or not the fibres need to be **blended**.

Scouring
This process is used on raw wool to remove the dirt and lanolin.

Carbonising
Vegetable matter is removed from the fleece by treating it with acid, heat and the pressure of rollers.

Dusting
This is needed to blow the dust out of the fibres and is particularly important in cotton production.

Blending
This is traditionally done before carding. Fibres such as wool and cotton are blended to ensure uniformity of colour and quality. For example, short fibres combed out during the **worsted** process may be blended with scoured wool from the **woollen system**. Lubricants are added to prevent the build-up of static electricity.

Fibres are mixed to produce different qualities of yarn. The spinner will decide the best way to achieve the required qualities. Yarns made of different fibres are known as **blends**.

The possibilities for blending fibres are infinite, but two of the most common combinations are wool/acrylic and polycotton.

❭ *Wool/acrylic*. Wool is more expensive than acrylic, a synthetic fibre. The wool is therefore blended with acrylic fibre to reduce the cost of the fabric.

❭ *Polycotton*. Polyester is not absorbent whereas cotton is. The two are mixed to produce a fabric which dries more quickly than cotton but is still absorbent enough to be comfortable next to the skin, as garments or as sheets, pillowcases and duvet covers. Polyester makes the fabric more durable than cotton.

Processes in spinning, from fibre to yarn.

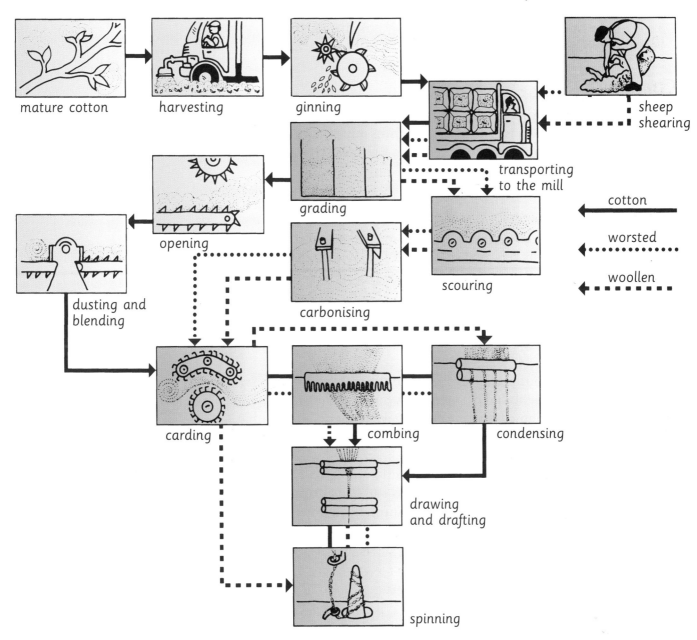

mature cotton — harvesting — ginning — sheep shearing — transporting to the mill — grading — opening — dusting and blending — scouring — carbonising — cotton — worsted — woollen — carding — combing — condensing — drawing and drafting — spinning

Carding

Staple fibres such as cotton, wool and acrylics are opened and loosened. They are then combed with a wire brush to untangle the fibres and form a continuous, thin, untwisted **wad** which can be spun. (If the fibre is a filament, the carding process is not necessary.)

In the woollen system, the final section of the carding machine divides the fibres into strips to form **slubs**. These are wound onto bobbins ready for **spinning**.

The manufacture of worsted, cotton and linen cloth needs additional procedures – gilling, combing, drawing and spinning.

Gilling

Gilling aligns the different blends together by passing them through a series of short-toothed combs. This prepares the fibre for combing.

Combing

Combing is a continuation of the gilling process but uses a finer-toothed roller comb. This process is crucial as it removes any remaining impurities and any short, broken fibres from the **sliver**. The remaining fibre is then wound into balls called 'top'.

Drawing

Drawing divides the 'top' further into a suitable thickness ready for spinning. This is usually repeated several times to reduce the top and to add a small amount of twist to strengthen the fibre. The reduced sliver is now called a **roving**. (Yarn in this state can be used in weaving, as it is in some of the less expensive cotton cloth.)

Spinning

The fibres are drawn out between rollers and twisted into thread. Yarns may be used as a single strand or plied by twisting strands together. Technology has contributed to some major developments in spinning, including the Sirospun yarn spinning system. Since its release in 1980, more than 150 000 spindles worldwide have been fitted with Sirospun. The process is especially suited to the production of lightweight, trans-seasonal, 'cool wool'-type fabrics. The process can be performed with only minor changes to conventional ring-spinning equipment, and with substantial cost-savings.

Find out more about this process.

Worsted yarn

Worsted yarns are made from long-staple fibres of the same length. They are fine, firm and highly twisted and give a smooth surface to fabrics. The fabrics are durable, hold creases well, soil very easily and are usually woven in a twill weave. Examples of worsted fabrics are the firmer, smarter dress materials, and wool for knitting socks. They are mainly used for suiting fabrics and other tailoring materials that require a smooth finish. Worsted yarns require more processes to align the fibres, which is why they are generally more expensive than woollen yarns.

Woollen yarn

The woollen system uses short fibres of different lengths to produce soft, lightly twisted, bulky yarns with protruding fibres that make them springy to handle and give a fuzzy or rough appearance. These yarns are not so durable as worsted yarns, won't hold creases, are easily soiled and easy to clean. Woollen yarns are less expensive than worsted yarns. They are used for knitting, and in woollen fabrics such as tweeds, flannel and blankets.

Silk yarn

The cocoons are sorted into categories.

> Those that produce the sturdiest cocoons are allowed to become moths and produce the next generation of silkworms.

> Those with sturdy cocoons will probably have produced from 450 to 1800 metres of continuous filament.

> The least dense cocoons are produced by the weakest silkworms. These are referred to by the silkworm farmers as being 'sickly'. These silkworms may have died before completing the cocoon or may just not be strong enough to keep going without a break. This silk is used for noil spinning.

> Deformed cocoons and those whose filaments are tangled between two cocoons are made into a coarse, slubby thread and are used to make **dupion**.

Categories of silkworm.

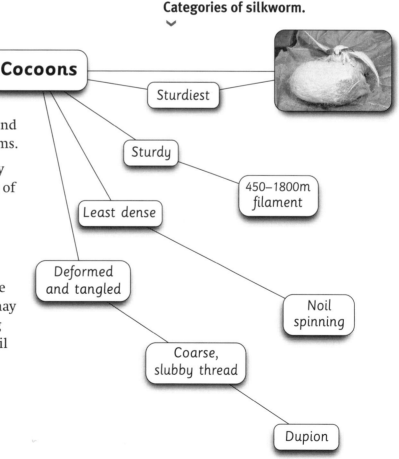

Cocoons — Sturdiest

Sturdy — 450–1800m filament

Least dense

Deformed and tangled

Noil spinning

Coarse, slubby thread

Dupion

The silk cocoons are de-gummed by placing them in a bath of water which is nearly boiling. The ends of the filaments are caught in a fine brush and the cocoons are unwound in a process known as **reeling**. The length of each filament varies from 450 to 1800 metres. The reeled silk is used for weaving but may need to be spun for making embroidery threads and heavier fabrics. Waste from the reeling process is used in noil spinning.

Continuous filaments

Synthetic fibres have copied the way that the silkworm produces its filament. All are made by extruding chemicals or dissolved cellulose through **spinnerets**. The fibres can be twisted as soon as they are formed to give a long smooth yarn, or they can be cut into staples for use in noil spinning.

Industrial spinning.

Woven fabrics

Fabrics, with the exception of felt, some lace, and net, are either woven or knitted. Woven fabrics are made on looms by **weaving**.

The warp must be very strong but the strength of the weave can vary to provide the appropriate texture. There are many different types of weave but they are all based on three things:

> the thickness of the yarn,
> length over and under,
> the type of loom used.

Weaving was originally done on small hand looms. Now, much larger and more efficient looms allow more varied fabrics to be made at a much faster rate.

There are three fundamental weaves on which all others are based: plain, twill, and satin. It is important that you become familiar with the many kinds of material available. Aim to collect as many samples of each as possible.

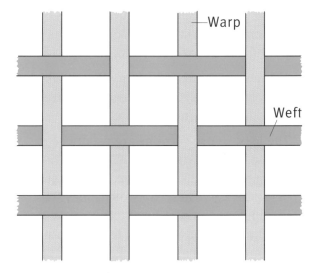

Warp and weft threads.

Plain weave

Lawn, gingham, organdy, chintz and handkerchief linen are examples of plain weave. These fabrics are generally strong and durable due to their firm construction as they are closely woven to produce maximum interlacing. There is no right or wrong side unless they are printed or specially finished. Possible variations are basket weave and rib weave.

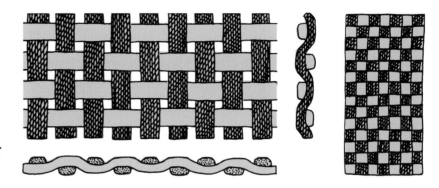

Twill weave

Cotton drill, denim, flannelette, woollens, worsted, gabardine, serge and some suiting fabrics are examples of twill weave. Twill always shows diagonal ridges across the fabric which can run from left to right or, like most cotton twills, from right to left. Twills have increased bulk, warmth and strength because of the closeness of the warp threads. This makes them great for work and sport. Twill fabrics have a right side and a wrong side. Variations of twill weave are Herringbone and Birdseye.

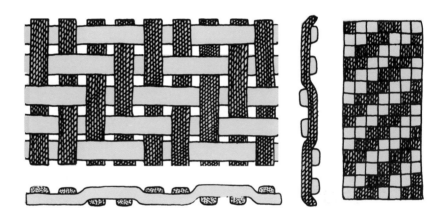

Satin weave

Satin weave is quite irregular and characterised by long, floating warp yarns lying on the surface of the right side of the fabric. These threads are called **floats**. Obviously, the longer the floats the less durable the material, as they tend to catch or snag on rough surfaces. It is these long floating threads that catch the light and give satin its characteristic shiny appearance. Silk and rayon are the most common fibres used for this process.

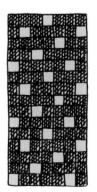

Decorative use of weaves

Yarn of different colours and textures can be woven to produce very attractive patterns.

› Woollens and worsteds are often woven into tweeds, stripes and plaids.

› Silks and silky yarns are woven into plaids, stripes and highly-patterned Jacquard fabrics.

› Shot silk is produced by using one colour for the warp yarns and a second colour for the weft. These give interesting colour effects when they are draped.

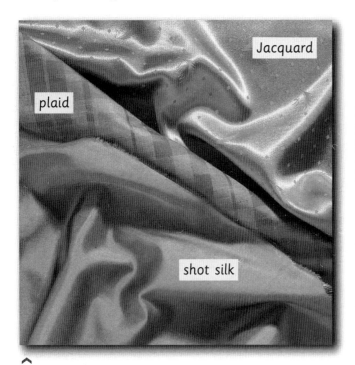

Decorative weaves.

Other woven fabrics

Flannel uses either worsted or woollen yarns woven using a plain or twill weave. A finishing process called **milling** brushes the fabric to raise the fibre ends. This fabric is quite soft and is commonly used today for nightwear and babies' clothing.

Crêpe has a crinkled appearance and is made using highly twisted wool or worsted yarns which allows it to spring and drape exceptionally well.

Tweed is well-known and popular for its hard-wearing woven woollen cloth. It is used for suits and coats.

Knitted fabrics

Knitting is a quick and cheap form of fabric construction and can use either natural or synthetic fibres. Knitting is the second most important way of making fabric. In simple terms, it is the construction of fabric by forming loops of yarn with needles and drawing new loops through the previous ones. It uses one piece of yarn and produces an elastic, stretchable fabric. Knitwear is usually made on large knitting machines, but knitting is still a craft in its own right. Creative original knitted jumpers are available. Hand knitting requires simple resources and so it is often used for making soft toys.

Generally, knitted fabrics are very comfortable, crease-resistant and allow body movement. They are elastic, 'breathe well' and are light yet warm. Knitted fabrics do not fray and don't require seam neatening.

There are two basic structures – **weft knit** and **warp knit** – which require different machinery and produce different types of fabrics.

Simple creative knitting.

Weft knit

Weft knitting has a longer history and tradition than warp knitting. It requires a single yarn to travel horizontally making a row of loops into which the following row of loops are knitted (as in hand knitting). Weft knitting can produce flat, circular or tubular pieces or complete garments that only require one or two seams to complete.

Three basic stitches are used to make weft-knitted fabrics: plain, rib and purl.

Plain uses one set of needles, either flat or circular, and is used for jumpers, hosiery and underwear. It ladders easily unless it is specially constructed. Plain refers to the *stitch* and not to the pattern of the *fabric* – Fair Isle knitting uses a plain stitch.

Rib uses two sets of needles which allows a greater variety in fabric design, particularly if the needles are placed at right-angles to each other. Rib has greater elasticity widthways and is therefore used for socks and underwear as well as wrist and neck bands on jumpers.

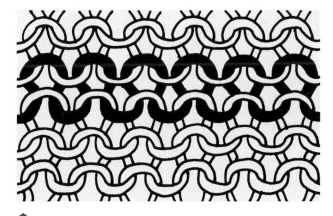

Weft knitting.

Purl is a combination of both plain and rib stitches, using either a flat or circular machine. Purl has elastic properties lengthwise and crosswise. It is used in children's wear, such as jumpers.

Warp knitting

Warp knitting has only existed since the 1960s. It differs in appearance and method of manufacture from weft knitting. Several hundred to over one thousand yarns are inter-looped vertically (warp direction) into adjacent yarns to form a flat fabric with straight edges. Warp knitting gives very stable knitted structures which are elastic and resistant to running and creases.

Examples of warp-knitted fabrics include tricot, which is used for underwear and other support garments, lingerie and swimwear. Cire (nylon tricot) is very shiny and smooth with a wet-look surface used to imitate leather. Warp knitting is often used for the construction of net or lace curtains, machine crochet and all kinds of lace.

Warp knitting.

A painting on bark cloth by native Mexicans.

Other fabrics

Felt is made from fibres, usually of wool, which are laid in layers. Each layer of fibres is at right-angles to the previous layer. The layers are washed and, as they dry, they become matted together to form felt.

For centuries **bark cloth** has been made in South America, Africa and Polynesia from the bark of trees belonging to the mulberry family. The process used is similar to that used for felt. It is possible to produce a very fine fabric but today it is mostly used for producing bark-cloth paintings which are sold to tourists.

Vilene® is a non-woven fabric made from synthetic fibres and is used as an interfacing or a strengthener for various textile products. **Wadding** is made in much the same way as felt but it is loose and springy and is not allowed to become matted.

Carpet weaving

Carpet making is an important part of the British textile industry. The backing of carpets is usually woven from **jute** and the pile is made from wool or from a synthetic fibre that has similar qualities to wool. There are many methods of carpet weaving.

Lace making

Lace is traditionally made from cotton or silk. It was made by hand in many parts of Britain until the mid-nineteenth century. It is now made by machine – Nottingham is the centre of commercial lace production.

Leather

Leather is made from animal hides by a process called tanning. Although you may not think of it as a textile, it is used in the same way as textile fabrics. It is most often used for accessories such as shoes and bags.

Extending your database

You should now be able to add records to your database about some of the fabrics that you have read about in this chapter. You will also need to add more qualities of fabrics.

Example of a database record.

Summary

You should now understand:

> how fibres are processed,

> the need to combine fibres,

> how textiles are constructed, especially woven and knitted textiles.

Activities

The work from these activities should be neatly presented and kept in your workfolder for future reference.

1 Look at some raw wool from a craft shop and try carding and spinning it.

2 Drop a silk cocoon into hot water. Leave it until it has sunk and see if you can find the end.

3 Look at different yarns under a microscope. Make drawings to show the main differences between yarns of different textures. Mount your sample next to the drawings and write a clear evaluation of each fibre.

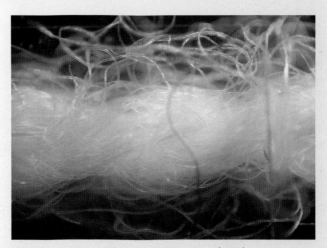

Woollen yarn under a microscope (x20).

Activities

4 You can work out different weave patterns in the following way.

Take two 150 mm squares of paper in contrasting colours. Draw a margin round one sheet and divide the centre into 10 mm strips. Cut along the lines but do not cut into the border. This provides you with a 'warp'.

Cut the second sheet into 10 mm strips and use it to weave a pattern on your 'warp'.

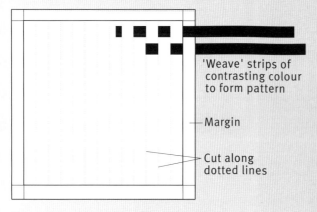

How to cut the paper for weaving.

Alternatively, you may be able to use a computer with a program that is specially made for designing weaving patterns.
You should find it easy to change the colours.

You may not be able to obtain a printout of your patterns if you do not have a colour printer or if your computer is linked to a loom. You can record your patterns by colouring on squared paper.

5 Look at these knitting patterns.

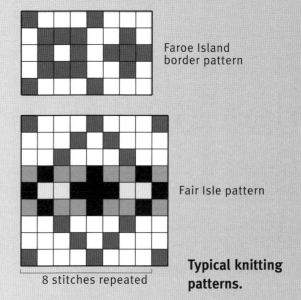

Typical knitting patterns.

Design a pattern that can be hand-knitted with two colours of yarn. If you do a simple geometric pattern you can show how it can be repeated to give an all-over design.

Questions

1 Why does raw wool fibre need to be scoured?

2 Why does cotton need to be dusted?

3 What is removed from the wool by the carbonisation process?

4 What is meant by carding?

5 Briefly describe the reeling process.

6 Which weave would you use to produce:
  a a firm fabric,
  b a thick fabric,
  c a herringbone pattern,
  d a shiny fabric?

7 In weaving, which threads form:
  a the warp,
  b the weft?

8 What qualities make warp-knitted fabrics more comfortable?

9 Why is Vilene® useful?

10 What are the advantages of combining:
  a polyester fibre and cotton,
  b acrylic fibre and wool,
  c cotton and Lycra®?

3 Enhancement of fabrics

There are many ways of improving the fabric so that it meets the demands of particular specifications. Some of the methods have been used for centuries but new ones are being invented all the time. All the methods described here are used commercially but many of them can be applied in the classroom or at home. Before trying any of these techniques, make sure that you:

> read the manufacturer's instructions,
> have permission from a responsible adult.

Consider whether or not you need to:

> cover all surfaces with polythene or newspaper,
> have an ample supply of running water,
> wear rubber gloves and protective clothing,
> wear goggles.

Dyes must be treated with particular care.

This chapter focuses on:

> how fabrics can be combined to improve handling, appearance and performance,
> how colour can be added to fabrics,
> surface decoration techniques,
> finishes for fabrics.

Combining fabrics

Quilting

Layers of fabric are joined together by sewing. The top layer of the fabric is usually selected for its attractive appearance, the middle layer or layers for warmth, and the bottom layer is usually very supple. The better-known uses are:

> anoraks, sleeping bags, etc. which have a hardwearing outer fabric, a wadding inner and a thin lining,

❯ patchwork quilts where the outer layer is made of colourful patchwork designs, the inner of wadding and the lining of fine cotton.

Decorative quilting uses a plain outer layer, wadding and a plain lining. The stitchery used to sew the layers together is done in beautiful shapes. In India, old saris – the traditional dress – are cut into suitable pieces and layers of fabric are sewn together using simple designs. Because the fabrics are very fine, the colours of the underneath layers shine through to give very interesting effects. The resulting fabric is used as a bed cover.

Quilting layers of fabric allows air to be trapped between the layers. This provides insulation. The insulation value increases if the layers used are good insulators.

Wadding is used for insulation, but it is not sufficiently strong or durable to be used on its own. It is most commonly quilted with a nylon lining, which is strong and flexible, and an attractive outer layer which is durable. The finished fabric is used to make items such as warm outdoor clothing.

Laminating and bonding

The improvement in fabric adhesives means that it is possible to bond layers of fabric to form a laminate. This is more effective than stitching as the act of piercing fabric with stitching creates lines of weakness. Laminates are being used increasingly to produce specialist sportswear, particularly for outdoor pursuits.

GORE-TEX® is a waterproof, breathable fabric which has three layers:

❯ a sturdy outer layer,

❯ a microporous membrane that allows perspiration to pass out but does not allow rain to penetrate,

❯ wicking tricot mesh inners which have a supple feel.

These layers are laminated together so that the wearer benefits from all three layers.

Plastics can be bonded onto closely woven cotton to give a firm waterproof fabric. If the plastic is bonded onto a loosely knitted fabric it will give a softer, more flexible fabric which simulates leather.

Adding colour to fabrics

Dyeing

Using dye is one of the oldest methods of adding colour to fabrics. You can dye the raw fibre, the yarn or the cloth. Dyes penetrate the fibre so that none of the original colour can be seen.

Safety first!

You should not use any dye without permission from an adult.

The earliest dyestuffs were made from boiling plant material such as madder and indigo. Indigo is grown, for example, in India and gives a strong navy colour. It was used with soda ash to create the first commercially produced dyes. There is now also a wide choice of chemical dyes.

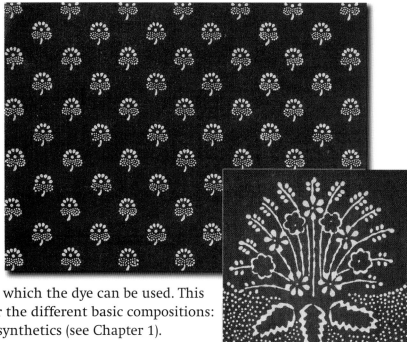

Dyes can be removed from fabrics by washing and by the effects of sunlight. When the fabric has been dyed, you want the colour to remain in the fabric. This quality is known as **dye-fastness**. The dyestuffs that are available always carry very clear instructions about the type of fabric on which the dye can be used. This is because different dyes are needed for the different basic compositions: cellulosic, proteinic and non-cellulosic synthetics (see Chapter 1).

Dyes are usually mixed with a fixative to give colour-fastness. Strong colours may still run if the fabric is not washed at a low temperature. The most damaging rays of the sun are ultraviolet rays, and chemicals which reflect these rays are used to reduce damage. All fabrics will fade if they are exposed to too much strong sunlight.

Czech folk cotton printed using indigo dye.

Random dyeing

Dye of the selected colour or colours is introduced by dripping it onto different areas of the yarn. When this is used for knitting or embroidery it produces interesting effects.

Random-dyed crochet cotton

Tie-dyeing

Tie-dyeing is a useful method for small items such as T-shirts, casual shirts and scatter cushions. (You can use it to give a new lease of life to an old T-shirt.) You can obtain a wide variety of colours and designs by simply tying parts of the fabric very tightly with string or rubber bands. You then dip the fabric into different dyes. The dye will only penetrate the fabric that isn't tied. If you are using more than one colour, you must remove the string and tie it in a different position before applying each colour. You can either dye your fabric *before* you cut out your garment or *after* it is completed.

Batik

Batik is another traditional method of dyeing fabric. Areas of pattern are worked using wax which resists the dye. With some of the complex patterns from Asia, the wax cracks and the dye runs through the cracks in a way that adds interest to the pattern. In Africa the method is used to produce simple, bold designs.

Stencils

A shape can be cut out in a piece of card. The card is laid on the fabric and dye is sprayed very lightly. The dye is applied to the fabric only on the area that isn't covered by the card.

Printing

With printing, colour covers the surface of the woven fabric. With fine fabrics, the colour may penetrate to the **reverse**, but usually there is a clear difference between the back and front of the material. Some fabrics are specially printed for further enhancement or decoration.

There are a number of options available if you wish to print fabric.

A printed fabric that was designed especially for quilting.

Silk screen printing

Silk screen is widely used for printing fabric and is particularly useful for small-scale production. Originally the method involved stretching a piece of sheer silk over a wooden frame. The pattern was drawn on the silk and then the area where the dye was not required was coated with several layers of a waterproof substance. Now, a very fine polyester fabric is used. The waterproof area can be created by applying a stencil emulsion directly to the selected area of the screen or by using a photosensitive emulsion. Fabric inks are available in many colours.

Roller printing

A printing block is prepared using the design. The dye or fabric ink is applied to the block with a roller and the design is then printed onto the fabric. For prototypes it may be possible to use a linocut for the block. Decorative rubber stamps are based on a similar idea.

Discharge printing

Discharge printing is used to apply a white pattern to coloured fabric. A bleaching agent is used to remove the colour from the cloth to produce the pattern.

Surface decoration techniques

Fabric painting

There is a very wide choice of fabric paints and felt-tip fabric pens in every colour for every type of fabric. These are used to create a design directly onto the fabric. Many of these can be sealed quite simply using a hot iron but some are a bit more complicated.

Transfers

You may think of transfers as the blue outline designs that are ironed on to fabric before working an embroidery pattern. This may still be a suitable option in some circumstances.

Patterns can be drawn and coloured in using special wax fabric crayons or the pattern can be painted using transfer dyes. The pattern can be transferred to fabrics containing polyester using a hot iron. This is the simplest and cheapest option for creating your prototypes and can result in a good-quality product if it is used as a base for embroidery.

You must not use other people's designs or photographs without their permission. If you want to use your own design, you can draw it using pens and paper or you can use a computer graphics program. You can use either of the following methods to transfer your design to the fabric.

> You can print your designs out onto Magic Transfer or Colour 'n' Wear sheets. You transfer the pattern to the fabric using a hot iron. The finished item can be washed using a low-temperature wash.

> You can transfer computer printouts, or photographs which you have produced yourself, to fabric using a specialised product such as Transfer-It or Colour Fun ImageMaker. The design must be very thoroughly covered with the Transfer-It or ImageMaker and stuck face down onto the fabric. It is then left for at least 24 hours, then heat-sealed with a warm iron. The paper is soaked with a sponge and very carefully rubbed away, leaving the ink layer stuck to the fabric. More Transfer-It or ImageMaker is painted over, paying particular attention to the edges of the image to ensure that it has stuck completely. It is then left to dry overnight.

A T-shirt with a printed transfer design.

Embroidery

Hand embroidery is still one of the most effective ways of producing a high-quality product, especially small gift items such as greetings cards, bags and decorated boxes.

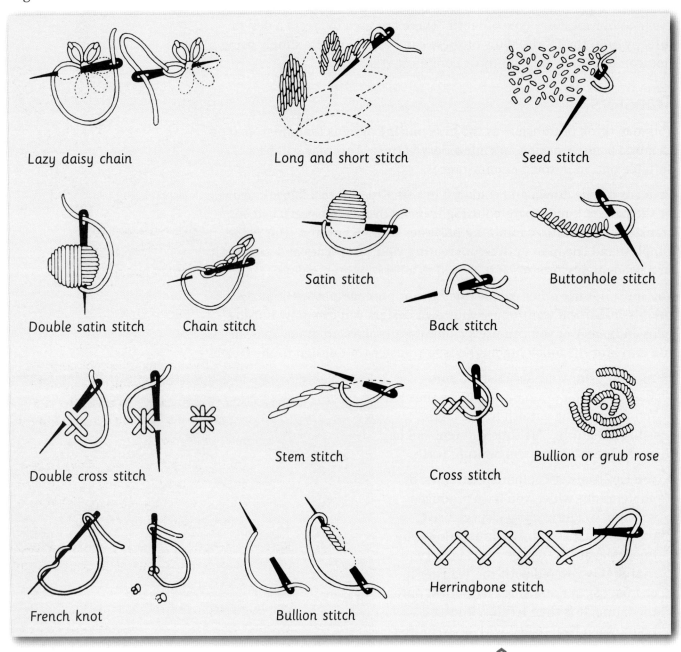

Embroidery stitches.

Machine embroidery can also be used. A sewing machine which is linked to a computer program can be used to produce beautiful small designs and logos.

Multiple-head sewing machines are used to produce repeat designs on the exotic silk fabrics which are displayed in the wedding section of fabric departments.

Appliqué

Appliqué, or applied work, is a wonderful technique for decorating textile products. A motif or shape is cut from one piece of fabric, placed onto another and stitched into place. The stitching can be decorative, worked by hand or done on the machine. Traditionally, appliqué is sewn with a machine satin stitch, but there is nothing to stop you using any of the many other stitches on your machine. Machine stitching is harder-wearing if you are making a product where this is important. Choose plain or patterned fabric and cut your motifs on the straight grain where possible to avoid stretching. Unless you are adding them to an existing item, apply the motifs before making up the garment.

❯ Cut a paper pattern for each shape.

❯ Pin the paper pattern onto the fabric and cut it out. No seam allowance is necessary. (Bondaweb is excellent to use when sewing appliqué. You simply cut out the shape from the Bondaweb and then iron the shape onto the garment. When heated, Bondaweb acts as a glue and saves tacking the shape into place.)

Sewing appliqué.

❯ Use a clear plastic embroidery foot on your machine and matching or contrasting thread to stitch around the outside edge using satin stitch to cover the raw edges. Watch that most of the stitching is on the applied fabric.

(It is quite difficult to sew round the edges of very intricate shapes. In this case you can use an iron-on polyester fabric called Funtex which does not need to be stitched.)

Reverse appliqué is produced by sewing two layers together and then cutting out areas of the top layer.

Beads and sequins can be applied to fabric. Traditionally these are sewn onto the fabric. Small pieces of bead glass can be welded to fabric using lasers which can melt either the glass or the fabric.

《 **Reverse appliqué design.**

Surface finishes

Fabrics can be treated with various finishes to make them resistant to fire, stains or creases. They can also be mothproofed or waterproofed.

Water-repellent finishes

Showerproof clothing is produced by using a close weave and then spraying the surface with a product such as Scotchguard™. At one time, the most common form of waterproof was oilcloth. This was made by coating fabric with layers of oil and allowing each layer to dry. Now plastic substances such as PVC and PVA are used to make fabric waterproof. **Waxing** is a traditional method of waterproofing and is applied to the finished garment. Cotton is used for this as it is absorbent and the heated wax can get right into the fibres where it is not easily removed. Some of the wax can be lost when the garment is cleaned but most dry-cleaners offer a re-waxing service.

Stain-resistant finishes

Products such as Scotchguard™ and Teflon® prevent stains from penetrating fabric and are very useful finishes for upholstery and furnishing fabrics.

Flame-retardant finishes

Most fabrics in everyday use burn very easily. Very complex chemical substances are used to reduce the risk of fire damage. One type is applied to prevent the fabric igniting. The second type prevents the flames from spreading once the fabric is alight (see Chapter 4).

Brushing

Brushing the surface of the fabric is a very old method of improving the insulation value. The teazles from plants were used to brush the surface of hand-knits to make them more fluffy. The teazle brush developed from this and now an industrialised version of this process is used to brush surfaces or undersides of fabrics to increase the warmth.

Degradability

Fabrics that will be durable but are able to be destroyed without causing damage to the environment are needed. Cellulosic and proteinic fibres can be destroyed by bacteria, fungi, mites and moths. Infestation by these can be avoided by keeping fibres clean and well-aired. To obtain a fabric that is easy to destroy, the minimum of protective finish should be used.

The Royal International Pavilion at Llangollen
is the largest insulated 'tent' in Britain. The
roof is made of three layers of PVA-coated
polyester supported on a 60 metre metal arch
that is 23 metres high at its highest point.

Fabrics are coated with PVA to make roller
blinds.

Yarns and fabrics are coated using metals so
that they glitter. These can be applied using
a number of different processes.

'Stainless steel emboss' by
designer Reiko Sudo:
splatter-plated polyester
taffeta.

Summary

You should now know about:

> how fabrics can be combined using quilting, interfacing, bonding
  and laminating,

> adding colour to fabrics using dyeing and printing,

> surface decoration techniques (fabric painting, transfers,
  embroidery, appliqué),

> surface finishes applied to fabrics.

Activities

The work from these activities should be attractively presented and kept in your workfolder.

1 Make small samples using as many of the decorative techniques described in this chapter as is sensible. You should find these enjoyable, so take care that you do not spend too much time on them.

2 Spray dyeing can produce very effective

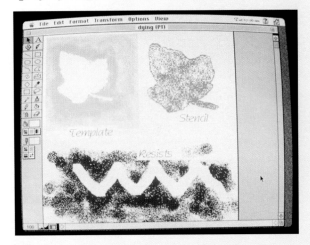

Computer screen showing simulations of dye techniques.

patterns but it can be very messy, particularly if there is insufficient space. It is easy to simulate spray dyeing using a paint program on the computer.
You can try it using patterns where you would use resists or stencils. If you are able to obtain printouts of the patterns, place them with samples from activity 1.

3 Some ladies' evening dresses are made with lots of beads and embroidery hand stitched onto them. It is now possible to produce similar styles without stitching. If you are able to find garments or fabric like this, examine them and see if you can think of a way in which it can be done. Many of the methods tend to be kept secret. Why is this?

4 PVA medium is used a great deal in textile work as an adhesive and as a water-repellent coating. It can also be used for creative work. Use it to stick a piece of polycotton onto a piece of strong card. Use fabric paints to add colour. Stick various fibres and fabrics onto this to make a picture or a pattern.

Questions

1 Name two natural dyestuffs.

2 Indigo was the first dyestuff to be used with a fixative. What was the name of the fixative?

3 You have obtained a dye for tie-dyeing cotton and find you have some left. Can you use this up on an article made of polyester?

4 Which of the following statements are true?
   a The right side and the reverse of the fabric are the same when the fabric is dyed.
   b The right side and the reverse of the fabric are the same when the fabric is printed.
   c Teflon® is used to make fabric a grey colour.

5 What is the name of the process for removing

colour from a dyed fabric to give a pattern?

6 Why are deep-dyed fabrics washed separately from pale shades?

7 A textile artist wants to use the transfer method to apply a design. Why must he/she use a mirror-image of the design?

8 Why are roller blinds coated with PVA?

9 Give the advantages and disadvantages of the following types of outdoor clothing:
   a quilting,
   b GORE-TEX®,
   c waxed cotton.

10 What are the advantages and disadvantages of making textile products that last forever?

4 Choosing fabrics for a purpose

It is important to understand fabrics and their properties so that you can choose them for the purpose for which they're most suitable.

This chapter focuses on:

> the properties of fabrics,

> British Standards for textiles,

> labelling and consumer rights legislation for textile products,

> care and maintenance of textile products.

The properties of fabrics

There is a relationship between the origin and structure of the fibres used to make a fabric and its physical properties. The method of construction can also affect the way a fabric behaves.

Basic properties include burning/flame retardance, solubility, elasticity and strength. Some tests, such as flammability tests, are carried out in commercial situations.

Flammability tests

Because of the danger of fire it is important that certain fabrics are flame resistant. The flammability of a fabric varies according to the way that it is used and the way that it is cleaned and so there are a number of tests for flammability – specific tests deal with specific situations. For example, upholstery fabrics may be tested to see how flammable they would be if a cigarette were dropped on them. The tests must be performed on the finished fabric because the finishing process may influence the result. For example, a fabric finished with a flame-retardant finish should not burn as quickly as one without the finish. These tests have to be done by independent laboratories to ensure that the results are valid, but firms will also do the tests in their own laboratories as part of their quality control.

You can investigate these properties by testing for yourself.

Flammability test.

Testing and evaluating fabrics

Where possible, it is best to relate your tests to your work. For example, if you are making a woollen jacket you may like to compare wool with a polyester blend for water absorbency, fire resistance and crease recovery. You could look at a local textile manufacturer and find out what tests it conducts to choose appropriate fabrics.

You might like to test some related materials or you may decide to run a series of tests to determine the suitability of a fabric with which you are unfamiliar. Modifications are often made to existing fabrics, which provides you with an excellent opportunity to test the old with the new and decide which is the best for your purposes. There are lots of suitable tests and you will find that the tests are quite enjoyable. You will also learn some interesting details about the materials you use.

Safety first!

It is important to check your proposed tests with your teacher before you begin so that she or he has the opportunity to approve your testing procedures. Discuss all aspects of the test and make sure that you understand the method clearly. When the purpose and procedure of your test are clear, you can begin.

Recording and reporting results

You could use the checklist here to write the reports from all the tests that you do. You may like to support your results with diagrams or graphs where appropriate.

Materials testing and evaluation: workshop testing activity report.
⌄

Heading	Notes
Materials tested	Give the names of the materials involved in the test. Describe the materials and identify their essential differences. Describe the specific characteristics being tested. Is this an appropriate test for these materials?
Purpose of the test	What are you attempting to prove? Comment on your predicted result. What criteria will you use to make judgements regarding the materials' suitability for a given situation? Why are these criteria suitable?
Description of the test	What method did you use for testing? Why did you use specific tools, equipment and machines? Briefly state your reasons for selecting your tools and equipment. Describe a possible alternative. Comment on the relative advantages and disadvantages of the alternatives. Why did you follow specific processes?

Heading	Notes
Results	Record all your observations and present them in an appropriate form. Ensure that your results are relevant to the stated aim of the test. How accurate were your observations?
Conclusions	Comment on the effectiveness of the tests and the actual result versus your prediction. Were your procedures appropriate? How do your results compare with other information relating to the materials tested? Could you repeat this test?
Recommendations	Give recommendations about the appropriateness of the materials for a given situation.
Resources	Be sure to attach a list of all the references you used for your report.

Procedures for tests

Burning test

The information here is adapted from an article by Carolyn Paulin of Victoria College, Rusden Campus, published in *Echo* Vol. 31 No. 1 1992.

Fibres, yarns and pieces of fabric can be used as specimens. If the product contains a combination or blend of fibres, test several threads from weft and warp to see if they have the same fibre content.

Safety first!

Care must be taken to prevent burning your fingers or inhaling smoke from the burning samples. You must wear protective goggles and a face mask. Hold the samples with a pair of tweezers. Do not allow any molten material to drop onto your skin. Use a protective mat to catch burning material. Be sure all material is cold before disposing of it.

> Describe the material before testing. What colour is it? What is its texture? Does it have an odour?

> Slowly move the fibre or yarn sample towards a small flame. Observe the reaction of the sample to the approaching flame. Does it ignite readily? Does it shrink away from the flame?

> Place the sample directly in the flame to determine its burning characteristics. How does it burn? Does it burn quickly? Does it go out quickly? Does it burn with melting? Is any smoke produced? Is there any odour that can be detected without removing the mask?

> Remove the sample from the flame and observe its behaviour. Is there an afterglow? Does it continue to burn? Does it continue to melt or smoke? Is there any odour that can be detected without removing the mask?

> Allow the sample to cool and check the characteristics of the residue. How does it smell? Does it resemble burnt paper? Does it resemble burnt hair? Can you crush the residue between your fingers?

Directions for the burning test

Unravel and test several yarns from the warp and the weft of the fabric to see if they have the same fibre content. Hold each yarn horizontally and feed it slowly through the edge of the flame of a taper. Repeat for a double check.

Fibre	When approaching flame	When in flame	After removal from flame	Odour	Residue
Cellulose Cotton Flax Rayon	Does not fuse or shrink from flame	Burns rapidly	Afterglow	Burning paper	Grey feathery smooth edge
Protein Silk Wool	Fuses and curls away from flame	Burns slowly	Self-extinguishing	Burning hair	Crushable black ash
Acetate	Fuses away from flame	Burns with melting	Continues to burn and melt	–	Brittle, hard black bead
Acrylic	Fuses away from flame	Burns with melting	Continues to burn and melt	–	Brittle, hard black bead
Nylon	Fuses and shrinks away from flame	Burns slowly with melting	Usually self-extinguishing	Celery-like	Hard grey bead
Polyester	Fuses and shrinks away from flame	Burns slowly with melting, black smoke	Usually self-extinguishing	Sweetish odour	Hard black bead
Elastane	Fuses but does not shrink from flame	Burns with melting	Continues to burn with melting	–	Soft black ash
Modacrylic		Does not burn		–	–

Creasing tests

For these tests you need three samples of each fabric cut into 100 mm squares. Use one sample of each of the fabrics for your test.

1 *Crease resistance*

> Take one piece of fabric in your hand and crease it up. Hold it in this position for 15 seconds.

> Release the fabric and observe whether the sample is creased. Record your results: no creases visible, some creases visible, very creased.

> You may be able to rate the fabrics on their recovery rate.

> Include the fabric samples in your report as part of your results.

2 *Ability to hold pressed creases*

> Make sure that your sample is smooth – iron if necessary.

> Fold to form a pleat and press well. You may need to use a steam iron or a damp cloth.

> Open the pleat and pull the cloth to see if the pleat holds. Record your observations.

3 *Creasing when washed*

> Wash the samples and hang them to dry using paperclips on a length of string. Record your observations as the samples dry.

> Try to iron the dry samples with a dry iron. Record the results.

> Take the samples that still need ironing and iron again using steam. Record the results.

Other properties

Insulation

It is possible to measure the insulation value of different materials to ensure that they are fit for the purpose. Continental quilts are made to keep you warm, and different people have different needs. Quilts are given tog values to show how much insulation they will give. Domestic oven gloves are used to prevent the cook from burning his or her hands and these must be made from a fabric that is not too bulky.

Acoustic factors

Furnishing fabrics absorb sounds and make a room much quieter. Carpets with a thick pile and curtains with a deep pile or texture are very good at absorbing sound. Sounds will be reflected from smooth surfaces.

Aesthetic qualities

Aesthetics are concerned with the feelings that different elements of design evoke. Some aspects are individual but some are much more general. Soft, cool colours are calming and can be used, for example, in the waiting areas of health centres and hospitals.

Comfort

For comfort, clothes need to be elastic. Generally speaking, knitted fabrics are most comfortable and thinner fabrics can fit like a second skin for activities such as aerobics.

Absorbency

Cellulosic fabrics are normally the most absorbent and the non-cellulosic synthetics are not absorbent. Towelling is usually made from cotton which is woven in a way that increases its ability to retain water.

Shrinkage

Fabrics need to be the same size and colour after they are washed as they were before washing. Fabric can be preshrunk and will not shrink if the laundering instructions are followed.

You can compare the information from these tests with the information in your database. Other important properties are: water retention, shrink resistance and strength.

British Standards for textiles

Standards of all textiles in the United Kingdom, including European standards, are delivered by the British Standards Institution (BSI). All standards are reviewed continually to take account of changing needs. The BSI provides:

> a large catalogue containing brief descriptions of all the standards, which you should find in the reference section of your main library,

> copies of the full standards, which are held in specialised libraries,

> glossaries so that manufacturers use words consistently to describe textiles goods.

Some products, for example nightwear, soft toys and furnishings, are required by law to meet certain standards of safety.

> In house fires, flammable sleepwear and dressing gowns are found to contribute significantly to the injuries. Fabrics and fabric combinations used in nightwear must comply with BS5722 to ensure that they will not ignite and burn easily. Since the type of detergent used in washing the garments can affect the flame retardance, very clear labelling is essential (see page 37).

> Since the application of a flame-retardant finish makes the clothing less comfortable to wear, different standards are needed for different purposes. (The potential discomfort has to be balanced against the risk.)

BS6249 includes a classification for flammability and durability to cleaning. Two test methods for firefighters' clothing are given in British Standard European Norms documents:

> BS EN 366 – a test for fabrics exposed to radiant heat.

> BS EN 367 – a test of heat transfer when exposed to flames.

Samples of the flame-retardant and resistant fabrics used are sent to independent test laboratories which will issue a certificate to fabrics that reach the approved standards.

> Soft toys must meet BS5665. The fillings must be clean and free from dust. The eyes and nose components must be safe and the fur fabric should be made to a given standard. If you are making soft toys, you are allowed to certify them yourself. You must keep a file for each kind of toy you make. You must include: diagrams of how the toy is constructed, details of the fabric, components and filling used and receipts of purchase which should show that the materials comply with BS5665.

Labelling and consumer rights legislation relating to textiles

Safety at work

Safety considerations are a matter of concern, both for the final product and for the manufacturing process. There is legislation to protect workers – the Safety at Work Act gives responsibility for safety to individuals at work to the employer and the workers.

Consumer rights

The Consumer Protection Act is intended to ensure that goods are fit for the purpose. The Trade Descriptions Act should ensure that the goods are correctly described. Each County or Regional Council in the UK employs a Trading Standards Officer who is responsible for ensuring that these laws are enforced. The Officers also give advice to manufacturers so that any pitfalls in the making and labelling of goods are avoided. They can give information about how and where goods can be tested.

Care and maintenance of textiles products

Most of the finishes that are applied to fabrics (see pages 28–29) will affect the care that needs to be given to the finished fabric. People are very particular about cleanliness and like garments that can be washed frequently and furnishings that do not stain. A great deal of time and money is spent on research to find the best way of retaining the fabric finishes.

Textile products normally carry labels which give the necessary information in a simple form. These are called International Textile Care Labels (ITCL). A simple, easy-to-follow code is used.

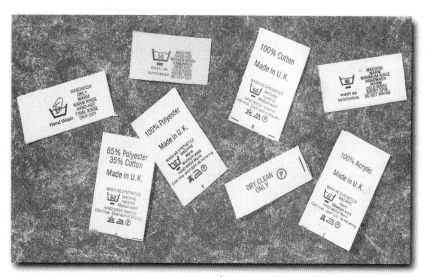

^
A selection of textile care labels.

The care label is usually stitched into a seam or is on a swing label. The ITCL code also appears on detergent packets (as you have seen, finishes can be damaged if the garment is washed incorrectly). **Ergonomic** studies show that the best position for the coded information is on or near the dials of the washing machine.

Summary

You should now know about:

> basic properties of fabrics,

> how to investigate fabric qualities,

> some British Standards for textiles,

> labelling and consumer rights legislation relating to textiles,

> care and maintenance of textile products.

Activities

1 On pages 33–34 there are simple tests that have been devised to show different qualities of fabrics. These tests are not standard ones, but they will give you some idea of the problems involved in testing. Make a record of the results. You may be able to add some of this information to your database. If you have more reliable information, you should put that into your database instead. Your information may be correct but the result of one test is never accepted as being reliable.

2 Design some tests to examine the effect of bleaches, dyes, detergents and fabric softeners on a range of fabrics.

3 Leave a small piece of pure silk in a solution of biological detergent and record any changes that you observe over a period of several days. Be sure to wear rubber gloves when handling the sample.

4 Choose a particular occupation and say what factors must be considered when providing the person with suitable clothing.

5 The British Standards Institution has a specification for domestic oven gloves. Design and carry out a survey to find out how many people know this. You must ask everyone the same question, for example:

Is there a British Standard for oven gloves?

You can work out the percentage of people in your sample who know about the Standard, either for the sample as a whole or for different age groups.

6 Discuss with others in your group the problem of ensuring that all nightwear is flame retardant.

7 Consider all the factors involved in choosing fabrics for each of the following garments:
   a a firefighter's jacket,
   b overalls for a firefighter entering a fire,
   c a baby's nappy,
   d a bobsleigh rider,
   e the staff in operating theatres.

Questions

1 Which fibre is used to make towelling?

2 You require trousers to have a very sharp crease. What fabric would you choose?

3 Textiles present a problem in house fires. Why aren't all textiles fireproof?

4 Make a list of garments which use a fabric containing Lycra®.
What are the advantages in using Lycra® in each case?

5 A café in a High Street has a small frontage but is quite long and narrow. There is a lot of noise from crockery and cutlery. In what ways could the use of textiles reduce the amount of noise?

6 If you were in doubt about the labelling for a product, who would you ask for advice?

7 Why must records be kept of the fillings and components of soft toys?

8 Draw the ITCL code for the following:
   a the temperature of the wash,
   b the temperature of the iron,
   c a fabric which cannot be bleached.

5 Influences on the design and manufacture of textile products

There are many reasons why people make textile products. Manufacturers have to decide whether a product:

> will meet consumers' demands,

> can be manufactured, marketed and sold at a profit.

Individuals often choose to make their own garments or soft furnishings when mass-produced goods are relatively inexpensive, for a number of reasons.

Some factors that could be considered are:

> cost,

> individuality,

> getting a good fit if you are not 'stock size',

> personal satisfaction from making something yourself.

This chapter looks in more detail at the influences which affect the design of textile products. It covers:

> how to research,

> how to design a questionnaire which could be used for market research,

> how to present your research data,

> the factors involved in consumer choice.

How to research

Research is a method of discovering. The key to research is to begin with a broad focus and work back to the details of your topic. If you follow these simple steps your results will be interesting and rewarding.

1 *Introduction*

> Clarify the topic.
  What are you investigating?
  Why are you investigating it?
  How is it related to design and technology?
  What do you already know about this topic?

> Are you doing an interview or a survey?
> Ensure that you formulate clear unbiased questions.
> Are you writing to companies for information?
> What specific information do you need?
> Where will you find it?
> How will you present your information?
> Will it be a written report, class demonstration, pictorial/graphic presentation or a role-play drama activity?

2 *Collection of data and information*

> ❯ Identify background information that could be relevant to your purpose.

> ❯ Read suggested reference material. Investigate primary sources of information (for example, interview and survey people, manufacturers and producers).

> ❯ Use secondary sources of information (for example newspapers, articles, reference books and journals).

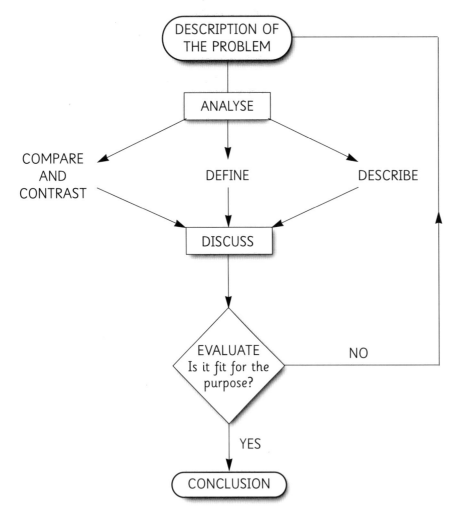

❮ **Flowchart of design analysis.**

3 *Analysis and interpretation of data*

> ❯ Analyse the data and relate it to your investigation. For example, what are the social, economic and environmental implications of the design? You must make sure that the information answers your initial questions.

> ❯ Check that you only select relevant information
> – don't get sidetracked.

> ❯ Have you everything you need?
> Do you need to look further?

4 *Conclusions*

> ❯ The reader will remember the conclusion, so make sure it has impact. The conclusions should draw the investigation together. Summarise your main findings. Do not introduce new information.

5 *Recommendations*

> ❯ Can you make any recommendations from the information you have gathered?

6 *References and resources*

> ❯ A list of all the references and resources you used must be attached to your work. People who have helped you should be listed under the heading 'Acknowledgements', and books and journals should be listed under the heading 'Bibliography'.

7 *Appendix*

> ❯ Attach an appendix of all primary data collected.
> This may include letters sent, copies of surveys, information sent to you and any other relevant information.

Where to find resources

Primary sources are personal interviews, surveys, questionnaires, photographs, drawings and pictures. Secondary sources include newspaper articles, encyclopaedias and abstracts. They are summaries of information from primary sources. You will need a combination of primary and secondary sources. The resources must be relevant to the aim of the investigation. You could consider:

> ❯ the manufacturer of the product,

> ❯ other related industries and competitors,

> ❯ conversations and interviews with teachers, family, class members and the wider community (over the phone, in person or through written questionnaires),

> ❯ your own observations,

> ❯ newspapers and magazines.

Producing a good questionnaire

Your questions must be easy to read. You can use either a word-processing or desk-top publishing package to produce an attractive questionnaire. When you use a computer system you can alter the layout without having to redo the whole questionnaire. It is easier to make sense of the information that you gather if the questions are as simple as possible.

> Questions with simple yes or no answers are the easiest to record.

> You could also use questions with a limited number of choices, or where the choices are placed in order of preference. Ratings are frequently used for market research. An example of such a question is shown opposite.

> This type of question is called a 'closed' question because it is not open to more than a limited number of answers.

> Open-ended questions are used to find out about people's opinions. The information from them is not as easy to interpret as that from the other methods. If you ask for the person's opinion of the proposed product at the end of the questionnaire, you may gain interesting information. Once people have answered the questions you will have some idea of the sort of information that is useful.

Do you wear jeans?	
Every day	☐
More than twice a week	☐
Once a week	☐
Less than once a week	☐
Never	☐

When you design a questionnaire you must ask for opinions about the questions to make sure that the questions:

> can be clearly understood,

> will not lead people to give the answer that you want them to give,

> will not give offence in any way,

> are likely to be answered honestly.

Some people tend to be naturally agreeable and answer 'yes' to questions and some are disagreeable and answer 'no'. The questioner needs to ensure balance in the way the questions are worded to account for this.

How to present your information

The main methods of presenting information are:

> written,

> graphic,

> oral,

> audio-visual,

> a combination of any or all of these methods.

Some will be more appropriate than others to different topics.

Written

You could use the headings given on pages 39–41 as a checklist to write a report about your investigation.

Graphic

You may be able to produce graphic information using the computer.
For example, imagine that you have obtained information to show that
a substantial number of people wear waistcoats and you have asked
a sample what fabric they would prefer from a choice of four.
You could record the results on a spreadsheet and then create
a chart of the information.

**Spreadsheet and pie chart
of waistcoat investigation.**

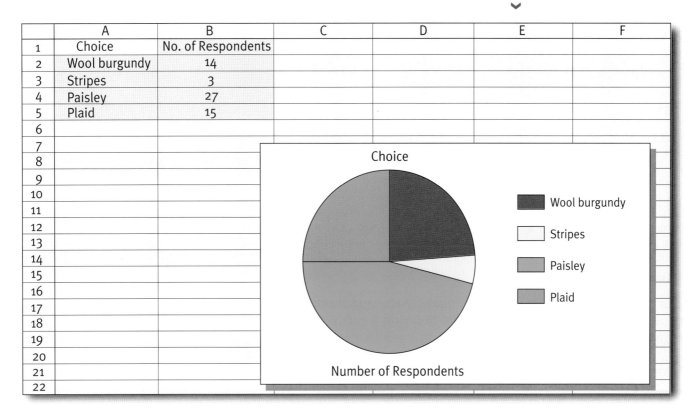

	A	B	C	D	E	F
1	Choice	No. of Respondents				
2	Wool burgundy	14				
3	Stripes	3				
4	Paisley	27				
5	Plaid	15				
6						
7						
8						
9						
10						
11						
12						
13						
14						
15						
16						
17						
18						
19						
20						
21						
22						

Choice

Wool burgundy
Stripes
Paisley
Plaid

Number of Respondents

Oral

You could give a presentation to your class about the results. Remember
to explain what you were trying to find out and why you investigated
this topic before you begin. You could use the headings on pages 39–41
to help you to prepare your presentation.

Audio-visual

You could include photographs and other materials in your
presentation. Remember to organise your material so that you don't
become muddled halfway through! Again, you could use the headings
on pages 39–41 to help you to prepare. Make sure that everyone can see
your visual material while you're speaking.

The factors involved in consumer choice

What you buy and how much you buy can be affected by the marketing strategies used. Think about those times when you have purchased something that initially you had no intention of buying. It is likely that the marketing of that product was one of the reasons why you purchased it. Some of the areas you might consider before buying a product are:

> safety,   > suitability,   > cleaning,
> defects,   > features,   > materials used,
> quality,   > price,   > care required.

Safety

You need to decide whether the product will be safe for your purposes. For example, if you are buying a toy for a very young child, you need to ensure that there are no small parts that could lead to choking.

Defects

You need to check that a product does not have any obvious defects. For example, both sides of a collar must match at the neck.

Quality

You need to check that a product is made to the quality that you would expect. You may check that seams and hems on a garment have been finished adequately and that there are no loose threads.

Suitability

You need to be sure that the product is suitable for your purpose. There is little point in buying a garment made in a heavy fabric for your 'holiday in the sun'!

Features

You need to look at the features of the product to see whether they match your needs. If a product has lots of buttons, it may not be suitable if you want to wear it to go to the leisure centre, where you'll need to change.

Price

You will be able to see at a glance whether or not you can afford to buy the product.

Cleaning, materials used, care required

You need to look at the care label to see whether you will be able to care for the garment without outside help.

Summary

You should now know:

❯ how to research,

❯ how to design a questionnaire,

❯ how to present your results,

❯ about the factors involved in consumer choice.

Activities

1 To find out what is already available you could attend trade exhibitions at which manufacturers display their new products. Find out about one exhibition centre and the exhibitions held there. Make a list of exhibitions that are of interest to textile manufacturers.

2 Think of a product that you wish to make.
   a Design a questionnaire to test consumer reaction to the idea.
   b Where and how would you launch the product?

3 Articles giving information about goods are written in fashion and homemakers' magazines. They often seem to be advertising products. Find an article about a particular type of product, for example bed coverings or trouser fashions. How does this sort of article differ from advertisements?

4 Many manufacturers tell their customers about products using the Internet. If you keep information about your product using an **integrated package** for the database, spreadsheets, graphs and designs, you may be able to present these as a computer slide show. To do this, use the 'Slide show' facility, which you will probably find in the view menu.

Questions

1 When investigating, what are primary sources? Name three.

2 How should you finish off any investigation?

3 Name three methods of presenting the results of an investigation.

4 What is a bibliography? Why should you use one?

5 Why should you keep all the information from your investigations in the appendix?

6 Why are 'closed' questions most suitable for questionnaires?

7 What are the advantages of designing a questionnaire using a wordprocessor or desk-top publisher?

8 Look at the spreadsheet and chart on page 43.
   a How many people were questioned?
   b How many choices were offered?
   c Which was the most popular fabric?

6 How textile products are made

To understand how goods are made, you need to have a good knowledge of the equipment and processes that are normally used. This chapter looks at the basic techniques for making textile products and the various resources. It covers:

> disassembling,

> tools and equipment,

> basic construction techniques,

> fastenings,

> computer-aided manufacture.

Disassembling

One of the best ways of learning how to make quality products is to look at the best available, and mentally take it apart. Try to imagine what the manufacturer started with and what techniques were used. You can decide whether you think the product meets the needs of the intended users. If it doesn't, you can consider possible improvements and keep a note of these to help you when you come to design your own product.

You must not copy someone else's design – you are evaluating existing products in the hope that you will be able to make improvements. Manufacturers continually look at their competitors' products to see if they can do better.

Tools and equipment

The essential tools for making textile goods are a needle and a pair of scissors. Having cut out the fabric, the pieces are normally joined together with thread which is passed through the layers of cloth using a needle. This is true for both hand and machine sewing. When the needle pierces the cloth it inevitably causes some damage. You have to select a needle that is strong enough to pierce the cloth without breaking but will make as small a hole in the fabric as possible.

Machine sewing needles

The most commonly used needle is a number 14 universal which is used for fabrics of average weight. When you finish using a machine, always make sure that the number 14 needle is replaced as this is the most likely needle to be required.

The point of the needle is very carefully engineered to prevent damage and you have to discard a needle that is damaged in any way. The universal needle has a point which feels quite sharp, but is actually smooth and rounded and can be used for all the usual woven fabrics.

For knitted or stretch fabrics, it is preferable to use a needle that has a ballpoint that separates fibres without damaging them. For sewing denim, a jeans needle, which has a specially cut point that penetrates the hard, tightly woven fabric, is used.

For sewing leather, there is a skin needle which is more like a miniature knife. This splits the leather and can only be used with a long stitch as the stitches must not be too close together.

Machine sewing

Before starting, you need to check that:

> the correct size of needle is in the machine and that it is straight and in the central position,

> the correct thread is used, and that the same thread is on the bobbin as on top,

> the correct stitch length is used.

The sewing machine works very powerfully by a system of levers to force the needle through the fabric. It must be kept clean and oiled. The thread in the needle catches the thread on the bobbin and the two are locked together – see the diagram.

You need to take two offcuts of the fabric you intend to use and make a row of stitching to check the tension. If the lower thread appears on top of the fabric, the tension is too strong. If the upper thread appears on the underside of the fabric, the tension is too weak.

The tension has to be adjusted according to the instructions in the machine's manual. (Some machines can be difficult, so check with the owner or the teacher before fiddling with the tension.)

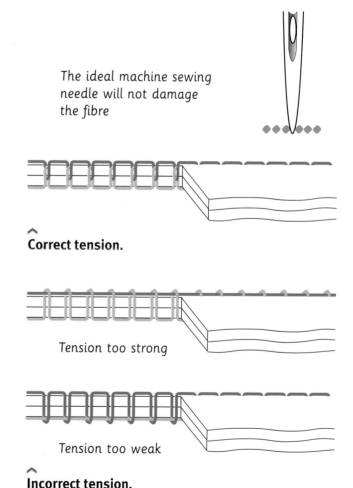

The ideal machine sewing needle will not damage the fibre

Correct tension.

Tension too strong

Tension too weak

Incorrect tension.

Linkers

Weft-knitted goods are assembled in mills using a machine called a **linker**, which uses a chain stitch similar to plain crochet to join the seams of garments. The use of the loop allows for a firm seam without losing the natural movement of the fabric.

Overlockers

The knit fabrics which are used for cut-and-sew products are warp knits. The stitches that are used are much too fine for a linker to be used, although a stitch with a loop is suitable for these fabrics. It is better if knits are finished with an oversewn edge. Machines have been developed that combine the benefits of a sewing machine with that of a linker.

An overlocking machine is used to cover the edges (over) with a locked stitch. The machine has up to four top threads but no bobbins for the lower thread. This part of the operation is again dealt with by loopers which form the loops that allow the finished stitch to stretch with the stretch of the fabric. On some models, the differential feed allows the fabric to move at the most suitable rate for the best result.

The knife on the overlocker trims off the surplus fabric as the stitching is taking place. It can normally be retracted when the stitching is not on the edge of the fabric. The distance from the seam line to the edges of the fabric can be controlled.

Domestic versions of the overlocker offer several options for stitching but an industrial model will probably perform only one stitch to a very high standard.

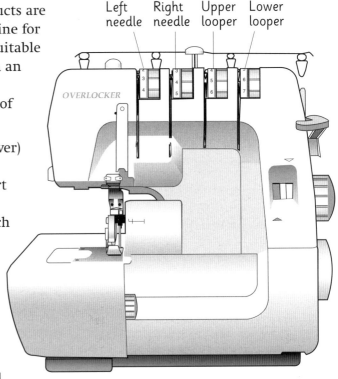

Left needle   Right needle   Upper looper   Lower looper

An overlocker.

Choosing the best stitch for the job

Although overlockers have been designed to meet the demand for sewing knitted fabrics, they are also used for woven fabrics. Many modern sewing machines have stitches which, though they do not form a loop, are suitable for knits. These are formed using a sequence including back and swing stitches.

To obtain the best result you have to use a sample of fabric. You should try the stitches that are available on the machines to which you have access. Only by comparing these can you know which is the best solution. If none of the machines provides a satisfactory stitch, then you have to choose a different fabric.

Scissors

> Sharp shears are used for cutting fabric. They must never be used for any other purpose.

> Paper scissors are used for cutting pattern paper.

> Small scissors with fine points that are used for embroidery will also double for cutting threads if you do not have weaver's/textile scissors.

> A buttonhole knife and seam ripper can be useful for making buttonholes and undoing seams but care is needed as it can also rip fabric easily.

Basic construction techniques

Seam construction

The line of stitching joining two or more pieces of f is called a seam. It is important that you are aware the various types of seam, their application to diffe fabrics, and their desired effect. You should choose appropriate seams for your product. You could use checklist to decide which type of seam to use on yo product.

This section illustrates some basic seam techniques you could use. If you require additional techniques your teacher or refer to a good sewing book.

Seam choice

> What type of product is being made?

> Is the fabric light and fine, or heavy?

> How will the fabric stand wear and tear?

> Is the fabric likely to fray?

> Is the fabric woven or knitted?

> Do you wish to emphasise the seam lines?

Flat seam

A flat seam is the most common and basic method of joining two pieces of woven fabric.

> Place two pieces of fabric right sides together, edges even, and pin in place.

> Sew 10–20 mm in from the edge, making sure that you stay exactly the same distance from the edge along the entire seam.

> Open the edges and press flat.

(Some fabrics melt at a low temperature. These can be joined by running a heated welding rod along a flat seam.)

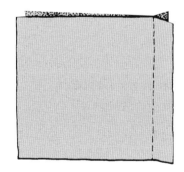
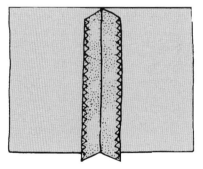

French seam

A French seam is usually used on fine, see-through fabric that is likely to fray badly. You usually use French seams for baby clothes, lingerie and some evening garments. French seams should be kept very narrow (no wider than 5 mm).

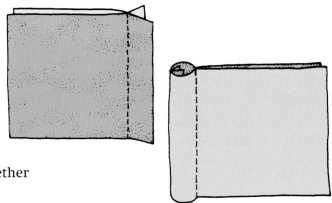

> Place two pieces of fabric wrong sides together.
> Stitch about 10 mm from the raw edges and trim both seam allowances to 3–5 mm.
> Fold the fabric over so that the right sides are together and ensure the seam is 'rolled' to the edge.
> Pin and stitch 5 mm from the edge.

Seam and fell

This is a useful neatening seam which is very secure and will not allow the fabric to fray. It is ideal for medium-weight fabrics such as cottons and linen. It is used on heavier fabrics such as tarpaulins and tents but can be too bulky for side seams for a denim skirt or tailored linen shorts. You could sew this seam in contrasting thread to make an interesting feature.

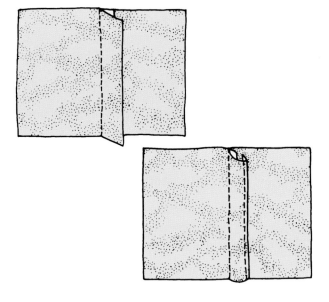

> Place the two pieces of fabric wrong sides together.
> Pin and stitch about 15 mm from raw edges.
> Trim back one seam allowance to 5 mm.
> Carefully fold the wider seam allowance in half, using the raw edge as a guide.
> Press the seam and carefully tack in place.
> Stitch along the fold.

Taped seam

A taped seam is really an extension of the flat seam and should be used in stress areas, or where the garment is likely to 'stretch' out of shape, for example the shoulder seam of a T-shirt. It is used when a woven fabric is cut on the bias.

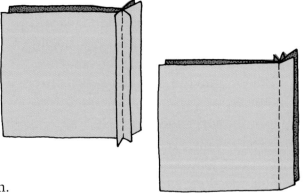

> Place two pieces of fabric with the right sides together.
> Pin and tack some seam binding or tape along the seam line.
> Stitch together carefully with the tape side facing down.

(An alternative method is to check whether seam tape can be threaded into the foot of your overlocker so it is sewn simultaneously with the seam.)

Piped seam

Piping is a very popular decoration technique in fashion garments, home furnishings and the upholstery in motor vehicles. You could think about using a matching or contrasting colour or even a printed fabric. A piped seam can be either soft or corded – depending on the effect you want.

> Cut 15 mm bias strips of the piping fabric as shown.

> Join them together to form a continuous strip or you can use commercially prepared bias binding.

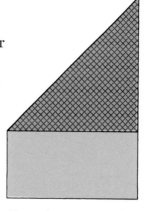
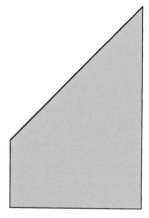

If you have a straight edge to your fabric, and you place this along the selvedge, the fold will be at 45°. Check by using a set-square or a quilter's ruler.

Cut along the fold. Rule lines using a fabric marker or tailor's chalk. For most piping, 30 mm (the width of a standard school ruler) is the most convenient width.

⌃
Cutting bias strips.

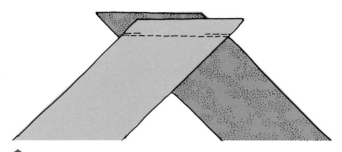

⌃
Joining bias strips.

Soft piping or tailored edge

> Fold the strip with the wrong sides together.

> Place the folded strip between the two layers of fabric (with the right sides together).

> Ensure all the edges are even and stitch through all the thicknesses.

> Trim away excess piping at each end of the seam.

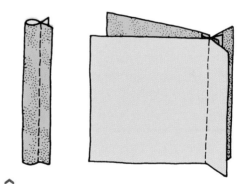

⌃
Piped seam.

Corded piping

Use the same technique as for a piped seam, but first fold your bias strip over cotton piping cord. Choose the thickness of cord that you wish and adjust the width of the strip accordingly. Corded piping is used to trim car seats, cushions, etc. and usually has a join. The join has to be as invisible as possible. Manufacturers take great care to have the join where it is least likely to be seen.

Stitch the piping first, using a zipper foot as close to the cord as possible. The needle position must be changed when the zipper foot is used. Continue as with the piped seam.

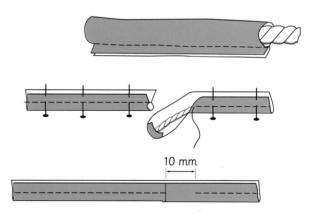

10 mm

⌃
Corded piping, and how to make a neat join.

Other techniques for seams

Wherever a seam curves, it should be trimmed and clipped to allow the seam to lie flat. In some cases, particularly when using heavier fabrics, you will have to grade the fabric to remove unwanted bulk. Some edges may need extra strengthening.

Notching

On the inside of a curve, always cut out small Vs, close to the stitching.

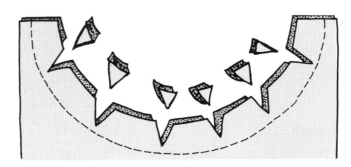

❮ **Notching.**

Clipping

On the outside of a curve, cut into the seam allowance, close to the stitching.

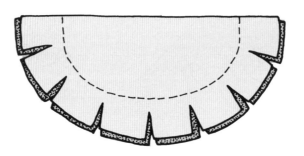

❮ **Clipping.**

Grading

When bulk needs to be eliminated, such as on waistbands, cuffs, and collars, you will need to grade the seam allowances. Trim the interfacing close to the stitching, then the under layer to approximately 3 mm, and the outer layer no greater than 5 mm off the stitching line.

Hems and edges

Straight-stitched hem

This is the simplest kind of hem. The edge of the fabric is turned over twice so that the raw edges are hidden. The fabric is ironed and then sewn with a straight stitch close to the fold.

Blind hems

If you do not wish the hem to show, you can use the blind hem stitch on your sewing machine or you can slip-stitch the hem by hand.

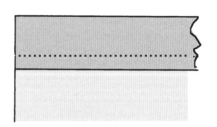

Decorative hems

It is possible to combine hemming with embroidery to give a decorative hem.

A simple hem.

Binding

Edges can be covered with bias binding. You may have a special foot for your sewing machine to make this task easier.

Braids and trims

Braids can be applied to hide the straight stitching or to cover the tacks or staples used on the edges of upholstery.

Pressing

You should press your product at each stage to ensure that it is well finished. Make sure that the iron, or press, is at the correct temperature. We normally press products to give them a smooth, flat finish, but sometimes we use steam pressing to form fabric into a desired shape. This method is commonly used when making hats.

Fastenings

Zips

Zips are more than a functional fastening used in trousers and skirts – they can be added to jumpers, tunics and jackets for decoration. Zips are made in a variety of weights, materials and colours. Open-ended zips are often made from heavy nylon and will not rust from frequent washing. There are various types of zip, and different methods of inserting them into a garment. Here are three techniques that you are likely to use.

Centred zip

Centred zips are placed in the centre of a seam with equal amounts of fabric on both sides.

> Sew the seam up to where the zip will begin and work five or six stitches in reverse to ensure strength at the stress point of the end of the zip.

> Continue to sew the remaining seam using a longer stitch. This will make it easier to unpick after the zip is inserted.

> Press the neatened seam flat.

> Pin the zip in position, ensuring that the teeth are centred over the seam.

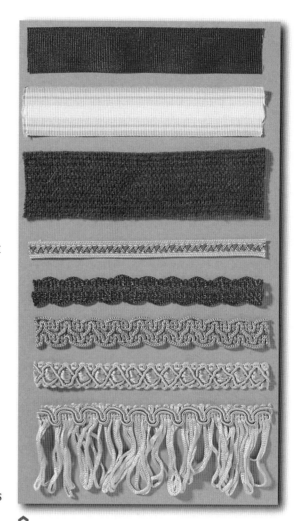

▲ **Some samples of braids and trims.**

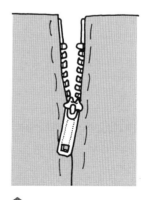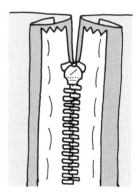

▲ **A centred zip.**

> Tack 5 mm from the zipper teeth and remove all the pins.
> Using a zipper foot, stitch close to the tacking on the right side. Start at the top and stitch down one side, pivoting (moving the working area round with the needle in the down position) at the corners and stitching back to the top.
> Remove the tacking.

Open-ended zip

Open-ended zips are usually centred with the teeth concealed like a standard centred zip. For a decorative effect, why not expose the teeth?

> Ensure that the raw edges are neatened.
> Pin and tack the seam allowance together along the fold line.
> Carefully pin the zip into position, either with the teeth centred over the seam, or with the teeth exposed.
> Tack into place 5 mm from the zip teeth and remove the pins.
> Using a zipper foot, stitch close to tacking but sew both sides in the same direction.
> Remove the tacking.

Lapped zip

A lapped zip lies behind a flap formed by the seam allowance on one side. Usually you would use a lapped zip on the side seam of a garment, for example a skirt or trousers. The flap usually faces towards the back of the garment.

> Ensure that the raw edges are neatened.
> Press the seam flat and then, working from the right side, place the zip under the seam opening.
> Pin and tack one edge close to the teeth of the zip.
> Lap the opposite seam allowance over the zip teeth.
> Make sure that the teeth cannot be seen.
> Pin and tack in position 10 mm from the fold.
> Stitch by machine as for a centred zip.

Buttons

Before you consider putting buttons onto anything, make sure that you can sew a strong neat buttonhole. It is worth learning how to do this as buttons can be very attractive and can greatly enhance a plain garment.

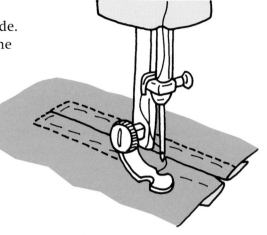

Using a zipper foot.

Decorative buttons. Choosing the right button is important.

Press fasteners

These come in a wide range of sizes and materials, and are used in garments, furnishings and industrial fabrics.

Belts, straps and buckles

These are very strong methods for holding things in position.

❮ A buckle on luggage.

Velcro shoe fastening.
❯

Velcro

This is a proprietary product which is strong and useful as a fastening and for sticking a fabric to a resistant material. A fabric strip which has nylon burrs clings to another strip which is velvety. It is available in sew-on and stick-on forms, or as a combination (one strip sticks and the other is sewn on).

Computer-aided manufacture (CAM)

Many processes in the mass production of textile products are controlled by computerised control systems. This has brought many benefits in speed, economy and safety.

One example is in the cutting out of fabric. In industry, the pieces for several products are often cut out at once. In the past, a very long, sharp, electrically powered knife was guided around the lines of the pattern by a worker, who was not always a skilled operator. Because of the sharpness of the knife and the value of the fabric, this was a dangerous and demanding job. This task is now performed automatically.

You should have the opportunity to see a computer linked to a sewing machine, or you may have the use of a computerised sewing machine which allows you to enter your own designs using a scanner. Computer-aided manufacture allows you to repeat a process many times. The software programs that come with these machines allow you to personalise textile goods by adding names or logos in embroidery. These systems give a very professional finish but you need to be sure that you are able to book sufficient time on the machine to be able to make good use of it. Plan exactly what you intend to do before making use of any resource, particularly those that are costly or scarce.

Summary

You should now know about:

› choosing materials,

› how to use tools and equipment safely,

› the fastenings that you could use on a textile product,

› how to neaten and finish your product,

› computer-aided manufacture,

› how to make your product.

Activities

You should keep the results of these activities in your workfolder.

1 Keep a record of all the needles that you use throughout the course and say why the choice of needle is so important. (Don't forget that machines cannot work without needles!)

2 Being able to thread a needle and not 'lose' the thread is an essential technique for sewing. What advice would you give to a beginner to ensure that he or she learns useful techniques?

3 Look at the construction of two garments or two items of soft furnishing that you own. To evaluate these, make a list of different techniques. Say whether you think the method chosen is the best and give reasons for your comments.

4 Make a collection of different machine stitches on a variety of fabrics and make notes of your observations of each.

5 Almost everyone has a textile product which causes them annoyance. Choose an item that causes frustration. Why was it made/bought? What features cause dissatisfaction? How could it be improved?

6 Look at a particular product which is available in a wide range of prices. What factors account for the price differences?

Questions

1 What type of seam would you use when making:
   a a winter skirt,   b a silk blouse?

2 What fabric would be most suitable for making pillowcases or a man's shirt?

3 Name three methods for fastening textile products.

4 When is a taped seam needed?

5 When would you use:
   a a centred zip,   b a lapped zip?

6 Where could piping be used other than on garments and home furnishings?

7 Why do many textile products need hems or binding?

8 Give two uses for Velcro.

9 Explain the difference between notching and clipping. When are these processes needed?

10 Explain how to eliminate bulk from areas such as waistbands, collars, cuffs and curtain pelmets.

7 Design

You should not need to redesign a product that works efficiently and looks effective. Designing has many parts. You are likely to have to design, trial, redesign and retrial many times to reach a final solution that suits the needs of the problem. You often need to compromise in one area in order to accommodate another and therefore achieve a balance. For example, a shirt may look best made from silk, but it would be too expensive. Therefore, rayon, a cheaper fabric which looks similar to silk, could be used. Good design is being able to achieve a balance between the various elements. For instance, the appearance may be the major consideration with less thought given to cost and function.

This chapter will focus on:

> basic design principles,

> ergonomics,

> aesthetics,

> recognising a need for design,

> the design brief,

> drawing up a specification,

> planning your project,

> generating design solutions,

> presenting design solutions,

> developing the design for making.

Creating balance. >

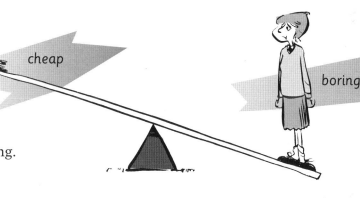

extravagant

expensive

cheap

boring

attractive

economical

Basic design principles

Elements of design.

Line

Line is a basic design element used to create style, shape, pattern, form and even texture. Different types of lines can have varying effects and meanings, and create different feelings.

Lines differ enormously according to character, direction, dimension and the relationship between the lines. Some more common lines are:

> vertical lines – these appear to add height, make something appear more narrow, and lead our eyes in an up–down direction,

> horizontal lines – these appear to shorten a shape or a figure, emphasise width, and imply solidity,

> diagonal lines – these take on the feel of horizontal or vertical lines depending on their slant and can add a sense of movement and instability,

> curved lines – these create a softened effect which can appear greater on a curved body or in the drape of a curtain.

Movement.

Direction    Pattern

Relationship    Dimension

Shape    Movement

Shape

Shape is made up of a series of lines or joined lines. The difference between shape and form is that shape is two-dimensional and form is three-dimensional. Different shapes create different feelings. For example:

> squares and rectangles add stability,

> circles give a feeling of movement.

Shape can be organic or natural (leaves for example) or geometric (precise). In clothing, you can look at shape in two ways:

> the overall shape of the garment,

> the shapes in fabric design.

Colour

Colour is a major factor to consider in design. It is, perhaps, the most obvious element and people react to it very strongly. Colour is known to have a psychological effect.

Primary colours

Red, yellow and blue are colours which cannot be made by mixing other colours. The pigments of these are needed to mix other colours.

Secondary colours

Orange, green, and violet are made by mixing two primary colours together:

> red and yellow gives orange,

> red and blue makes violet,

> blue and yellow makes green.

Extended secondary colours are those in between a primary and secondary colour, like red-orange and yellow-orange. These are often called tertiary colours.

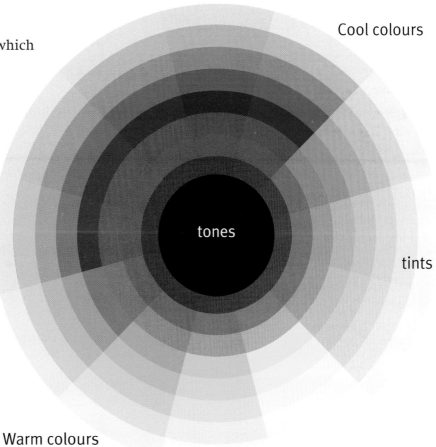

Colour wheel.

Cool colours

tones

tints

Warm colours

Tone

An added factor of colour is tone. Black and white fall into this category – both are referred to as tones rather than colours. We refer to black *shades* and white *tints*: a blackish-blue (or dark blue) is called a shade of blue, and a light blue is called a tint of blue. Black and white can be used extremely effectively in three ways:

> alone,

> with pure colours, for example, black, white, red and blue,

> mixed in with pure colours to make another colour, such as light blue and dark blue or dark red and light red (pink).

Don't forget grey. It is simply a tone.

Combining colours

Different combinations of colours will have quite varying effects. For instance, combining colours that are *next* to each other on the colour wheel gives quite a different overall effect from combining those that are *opposite*. There are thousands of combinations and you need to be careful that those you select suit the design of your garment or product.

Pattern

Pattern is a combination of lines or shapes which can be simple or complex, depending on the amount of detail used. Complex patterns are more detailed, but not necessarily better because of this. Patterns can also be regular or irregular. The intended use or application of the product is the major influence on the effect of the pattern.

Texture

Texture is the way the surface of something feels. There are two types of texture:

> real or tactile (the actual feel of the surface),

> simulated or visual (the appearance or look of the texture).

Texture can have a huge effect on the appearance of a product or garment. It must therefore be carefully considered in any design. For instance, a shiny surface will create a different effect from a fluffy or a harsh surface. In textiles, the feel of a material will determine how you can use it: a rough surface cannot be used next to the skin, while a slippery surface is inappropriate for a dining-room chair. You should consider carefully the suitability of a fabric's texture before using it.

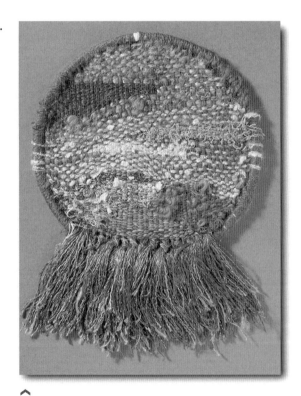

A piece of weaving to show different textures.

Ergonomics

Ergonomics is the study of the relationship between people and their working environment. When you design a product you are aiming to fulfil a need. Part of doing this is ensuring that the product can be used in its intended environment. You want the product to be comfortable, safe and efficient. Things such as the size of buttons and clasps must be considered and, in furnishings, things such as size and height. Ergonomics is more applicable to products such as home furnishings than to clothing.

Another word which is often mentioned when designing is **anthropometrics**, the measurement of the size and proportions of the human body. Anthropometrics is relevant when you are designing clothing.

Aesthetics

Aesthetics is the study of the nature of beauty. It relates to the visual aspects (those areas or things you see) of the product. The appearance of the product is important in marketing, particularly of textile designs and fashion products.

You often look at products and make judgements about them according to whether you like or dislike their appearance. However, remember that a judgement about appearance is very personal. To judge the aesthetics of a product objectively, it can be easier to break it into the elements of design: line, shape, form, pattern, texture, and colour.

There are two ways to assess the aesthetics of a product:

❭ through an aesthetics analysis,

❭ by looking at each of the elements of design.

One or both of these can be used. You could use the following checklist.

Aesthetics analysis

- Is it well made?
  Why?
  Why not?
- Is it a simple design?
- Does the design suit the material used?
- How much decoration is on it?
  Is the decoration suitable?
- What colour is it?
  Does the colour suit the intended purpose?
  Does it hang well?
- Will it show dirt easily?
- Will it be easy to clean?
- Will it crease easily?
- Does its design appear balanced?
  Are there any areas which don't blend in with the design?

Recognising a need for design

You can identify a need for a design in different ways. Here are some ideas:

> brainstorming,
> looking at existing products,
> written information,
> conversations with others about their needs.

Brainstorming

It is important to investigate a product before designing or redesigning. A good starting point is brainstorming. Brainstorming is a method of writing down and thinking about lots of ideas relating to the problem or project. Brainstorming is done as a group or class to generate lots of ideas, and is usually done in one of two ways.

1 **Through making comparisons**
   You relate a problem or product to something you already know and work from there.

2 **Enquiring**
   You may not know much or anything about the production or problems. You enquire – through people, books, resources of any sort – and use this as a starting point. It is a good idea to jot down ideas and words that come up while you are brainstorming as they can be useful in later stages of designing.

Brainstorming cushions.

Comfort

Cushions for seats

Movable

Fitted

Decoration

Shape

Multi-purpose

Easy to move

Cleaning?

Durability

Size

Methods of attachment

Once you have a range of ideas, you can examine them more thoroughly – in other words, do some research.

Looking at existing products

Consider any textile product that interests you. It will be better to choose a product that you are likely to make.

Function

Function is the purpose for which a product was designed. There are two ways of analysing a product's function.

❯ What is the product intended for?

❯ What other functions does it have, even though they aren't its intended use?

A chair, for example, is designed to be sat on – that is its function. But a chair has many other functions – for example to stand on, to pile books on, to hang clothes over!

When designing a product it is useful to complete a function analysis. This is not a difficult task and it helps your designing and allows you to find out more about the intended purpose of the product, which will enable you to explore more ideas. A function analysis is a list of questions related to the function of the product. Here is a list of questions that you could use. You may not wish to use all these questions for all products. There may be questions of your own you can add.

Function analysis

- What is it?
- What is its main purpose?
- Is it easy to see what its function is?
- What other things can it do or be used for?
- How does it do it?
- Identify each part of the product. What does each part do? Are there any parts that may wear?
- What care instructions are there? Are any needed?
- Is it safe? Are there any features which may not be safe?
- How long is it designed to last? Will it last this long?
- Are the selected materials appropriate?
- Who might use it?
- What is the historical development of the product?
- What alternatives could be used?
- Are there any unnecessary features?
- Is it good value for money?

Disassembling

Look at other products and decide whether you think the product meets the needs of the intended users. If it doesn't, you could redesign it so that it will.

You must not copy someone else's design. It would be unfair if someone spent a great deal of time developing a product and you came along and copied it, so there are laws to protect people's work.

Some basic designs, such as straight skirts or men's shirts, can be copied. In this case you can take an old garment apart and use it as a pattern for a new one. You would be using fabric and finishes of your own choice, so the overall design would be yours.

You should always acknowledge patterns and designs that are not your own.

Written information

Articles in magazines or published patterns may give you some ideas for your own designs. You should keep your eyes open for any materials that could be useful to you. For example, mail-order catalogues will often give size charts which you could use when designing your own products.

Conversations with others about their needs

A chance remark may lead you to a design idea. For example, a mother with a baby may say that some baby clothes are awkward to use because they don't have simple fastenings, or the fastenings do not make it easy to change a nappy. You could design a baby's garment that is easier to use.

The design brief

A design brief is a short, clear statement describing the need or problem. The brief must be outlined so that you have clear guidelines before you begin any project. If you are working for a client, he or she should check the brief carefully. A design brief may be given to you by a teacher or client and it is up to them to make sure that it is clearly set out. However, if you have to write your own brief, the main things you need to include are:

> a statement of the problem or project,

> a statement of the function of the product,

> a list of special considerations and limitations.

Always keep the brief simple and clear as you will need to refer back to it regularly.

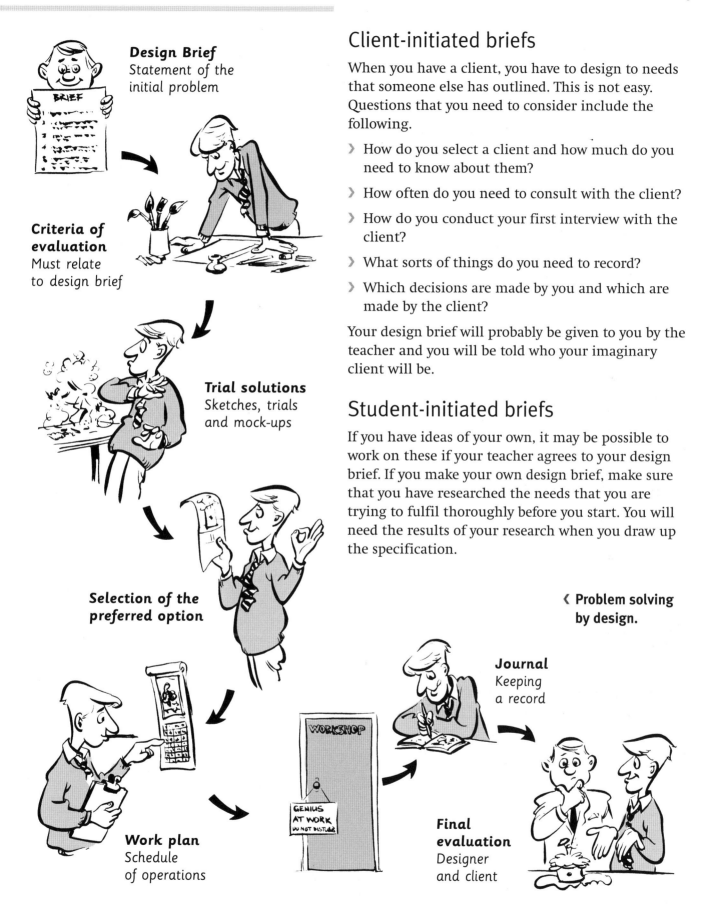

Design Brief
Statement of the
initial problem

**Criteria of
evaluation**
Must relate
to design brief

Trial solutions
Sketches, trials
and mock-ups

**Selection of the
preferred option**

Work plan
Schedule
of operations

Journal
Keeping
a record

**Final
evaluation**
Designer
and client

❮ **Problem solving
by design.**

Client-initiated briefs

When you have a client, you have to design to needs
that someone else has outlined. This is not easy.
Questions that you need to consider include the
following.

❯ How do you select a client and how much do you
  need to know about them?

❯ How often do you need to consult with the client?

❯ How do you conduct your first interview with the
  client?

❯ What sorts of things do you need to record?

❯ Which decisions are made by you and which are
  made by the client?

Your design brief will probably be given to you by the
teacher and you will be told who your imaginary
client will be.

Student-initiated briefs

If you have ideas of your own, it may be possible to
work on these if your teacher agrees to your design
brief. If you make your own design brief, make sure
that you have researched the needs that you are
trying to fulfil thoroughly before you start. You will
need the results of your research when you draw up
the specification.

Drawing up a specification

The specification should explain why you are designing the product and what it is supposed to do. You should include your research findings, such as how big the product needs to be, relevant anthropometric data, and any analysis of existing products. You should list constraints, such as time, resources and manufacturing requirements (for example, whether the product is a one-off item or would be mass-produced).

Planning your project

When designing, you should produce a design plan, which is sometimes called a sequence of events, production plan or a work plan. The design plan is a plan of your project and the steps you will follow, and provides:

❯ a timeline for your project,

❯ a breakdown of each task within your project.

It is important to break your work into small, achievable tasks. You may not follow your plan exactly, because you are constantly evaluating and reassessing tasks, but it is a starting point. You should keep a journal or log of your progress through the project as part of your plan.

You must explore different ideas and directions to make sure that you achieve the best result, which may not be (and often isn't) your original solution.

A design plan.

Task	Details	Date for completion
Formulating design brief	Consulting the client Outlining the problem Defining considerations and limitations	
Design plan	Planning time allowed Allocating time to tasks Formulating criteria for evaluation	
Trial solutions	Record and investigate Sketch possible solutions Make mock-ups Disassemble similar products	
Preferred solution	Selecting the preferred solution Client consultation Working drawings and plans Presentation drawings	
Work plan	Clearly outline the plan for production	

Task	Details	Date for completion
Production	Organising the pattern Cutting fabric Sewing main seams Neatening seams Decoration	
Journal	Regularly updating the processes followed	
Evaluation	Evaluating the final product Self (designer) evaluation Client evaluation User evaluation	

Generating design solutions

Once you have investigated an area thoroughly, you will have gained much background knowledge and be able to draw up a series of options. You will often gain ideas while investigating. Make sure you always put ideas down on paper – draw them! Your drawings can be rough thumbnail sketches. It is often good to use annotated drawings – that is, drawings that have explanatory notes.

First ideas for a sweatshirt.

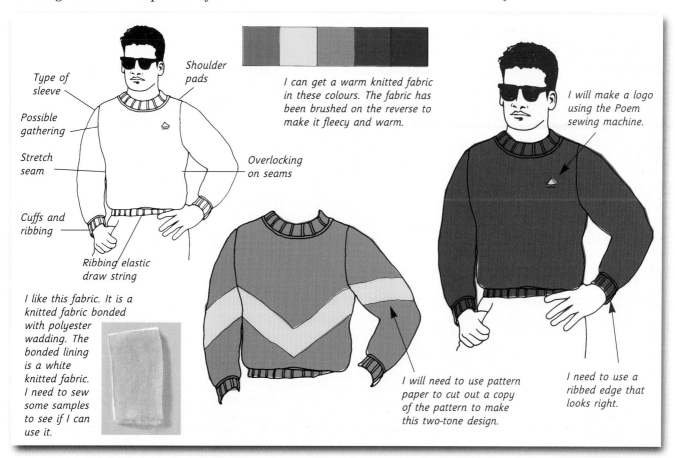

Type of sleeve

Shoulder pads

Possible gathering

Stretch seam

Cuffs and ribbing

Ribbing elastic draw string

I like this fabric. It is a knitted fabric bonded with polyester wadding. The bonded lining is a white knitted fabric. I need to sew some samples to see if I can use it.

I can get a warm knitted fabric in these colours. The fabric has been brushed on the reverse to make it fleecy and warm.

Overlocking on seams

I will make a logo using the Poem sewing machine.

I will need to use pattern paper to cut out a copy of the pattern to make this two-tone design.

I need to use a ribbed edge that looks right.

Presenting design solutions

You can present your design solutions using a combination of text, graphical techniques and computer-generated images.

Graphical techniques

Graphical techniques are used for two reasons:

> to sell your product indicating the 'look' of it, including shape, style and materials used,

> to show how it is made.

Different areas of technology use different types of drawings to show their products and ideas clearly. For textiles, you may need to draw a piece of furniture to show the textile covering or you may need to draw a garment. The two areas will require different approaches. The furniture will require you to complete a pictorial drawing, whereas the main emphasis in clothing will be on the figure. To complete a drawing of a figure, you will need to understand some basic rules about proportion. If you need to complete a series of garment drawings, complete one figure drawing and photocopy it several times. You can then 'dress' each figure as you wish.

To 'sell' your product

When you draw to 'sell' your product, you need to make it look realistic and appealing. This is often done through a technique called rendering. Rendering makes a drawing appear three-dimensional and shows tone and texture. Rendering can be done in many different ways and using different media. The materials you choose will depend on the effect you are after. You can use grey lead pencil, charcoal, crayons, pastels, markers, ink, paint, coloured pencils, airbrushing, watercolours, washes or fine-point markers. You can scan an outline of your drawing into a three-dimensional rendering program on a computer and give the computer instructions to complete your drawing.

Working drawings

Working drawings assist in the making of a product and therefore need to show details such as shape and size. If you were completing working drawings for something like a canvas chair, you would be most likely to use orthogonal drawings which show different views of the product. Sometimes this may also be accompanied by a sectional drawing.

In clothing, you are most interested in the cut and shape of the garment and each piece within the garment. The type of drawing you use needs to outline these factors.

Computer-aided design

You can use a computer-aided design program to create and manipulate a range of two-dimensional and three-dimensional images, produce accurate drawings and graphics.

Developing the design for making

When you have chosen your design solution to develop, you need to go through these stages.

› Test or trial your design so that you can make decisions about the material(s) to make it in, the critical dimensions and tolerances that will determine how you make your product, and what ready-made items you could use (for example, zips).

› Model the design so that you can find out how accurate your making up needs to be for the product to do what it is supposed to do.

› Make any changes to the design that are needed.

› Consider how the product might be made in quantity, as well as a one-off item.

Testing and trialling

It may be necessary to make samples or models to test before making the actual product. Prototypes, mock-ups and models are all methods of testing the materials, processes and equipment you wish to use. They are particularly important if you are using a new material, machine or processes as you cannot be sure of the result until you test it.

Samples

A sample usually tests one section of your product. For instance, you may need to test a variety of seams on a new fabric you want to use. To find a result, you only need to complete each type of seam once – you don't need to complete the whole garment. Another instance where you will usually need to complete at least one sample is in decoration. You don't need to complete the whole decorative piece, but you must test it to ensure that the method suits the fabric.

Keep all your samples. Even if the sample has not worked very well, it should be kept because you may come back to this idea later, or you may see how it can be improved. If you put an idea to one side and then look at it later, you can be much more objective.

People often work in a team in industry and these samples and ideas are pinned on a board so that everyone can see the progress. This board is called a storyboard.

A storyboard.

Mock-ups

A mock-up or model is usually a complete product but is often made using a different material. If the product is large, the mock-up may be a scale model of the product. Mock-ups and models are made to see what the shape, size, proportion and overall look will be.

In textiles, a mock-up of a garment may be made from calico or a cheap cotton fabric. If this is for a client you need to check that it is all right. A large company would have a customer panel to assess the prototypes. When you make something for yourself, you may like to have the advice of a trusted friend. If the product is part of examination coursework, the comments of your teacher are very valuable, even when they differ from those of friends!

Samples and testing are probably the areas you most like to avoid, as you usually want to move on to making the final product. But be careful – spending a little extra time at this stage will save a lot of time, effort and frustration.

Once you are satisfied that you have completed all the tests you need you are ready to make your final product.

Summary

You should now know:

› about the basic design principles of line, shape, colour, pattern and texture,
› about ergonomics and aesthetics,
› how to recognise a need for design, through brainstorming, looking at existing products, written and verbal information,
› what a design brief is and how to write one,

› how to draw up a design specification,
› how to plan your project,
› how to generate design solutions,
› how to present design solutions using graphical techniques, computer-aided design, and mock-ups,
› how to develop a design for making.

Activities

1 Collect pictures of textile garments and objects that show good use of the following (two examples per area):
   a line,   c shape,
   b colour combinations,   d pattern.

2 Select a product that you use regularly at home and answer the function analysis questions on page 63. Add at least two more questions of your own.

3 Think of two things you use every day that you find attractive or appealing and two that you don't. Explain why. See if you can redesign an unappealing object.

4 Write down as many uses as you can think of for a clothes peg.

5 Complete a simple line drawing of a product. Photocopy or trace it (manually or on the computer) three times on separate sheets,

and complete the following:
   a a function analysis,
   b an ergonomic analysis,
   c an aesthetics analysis.

Use the checklists on pages 61 and 63 to help you. You could produce an annotated drawing to show your results.

6 An example of a client-initiated design brief could be as follows.

Students at your school are forever complaining about hard chairs. Design something that will make the chairs more comfortable. Considerations and limitations include cost, the ability to be mass-produced, hardwearing, and stackable.

Draw up the design specification, the design plan, generate design solutions, and develop the design for making.

Questions

1 Name the primary colours.
2 Horizontal lines go up and down. True or false?
3 Name two 'cool' colours.
4 Which is used to tint, black or white?
5 Name the five elements of design.
6 Aesthetics is to do with the function of a product. True or false?

7 Ergonomics is the study of the relationship between people and their environment. True or false?
8 How would you render a drawing?
9 Explain what would be in a design brief. What is meant by 'creating a balance in design'?
10 What should you include in a design plan?

8 Production of textile items

This chapter focuses on:

> systems,

> the importance of good organisation and systematic working when manufacturing textile goods,

> types of production systems,

> case studies of textile production.

Systems

A system is a methodically arranged set of ideas and/or tools performing a specific process. For example, using a machine for sewing can be represented as the following system.

> **System diagram for using a machine for sewing.**

An organisation is made up of a number of systems linked in an organised way. It has a beginning and an end shown by boxes shaped like this:

> **Beginning/end box on a system flowchart.**

The system or the process is always shown on a flowchart as a rectangle. The people who work in one system know where the output from their particular system goes when it leaves them. They may have to make a decision. The decision is shown in a box that has a choice, like this:

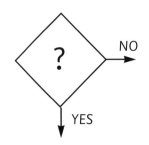

> **Decision box on a system flowchart.**

72

There are different decision boxes for more complex decisions and you can find these on a flowchart template. A typical flowchart for the manufacture of a textile product is shown here.

Flowchart for the production of a textile item.
⌄

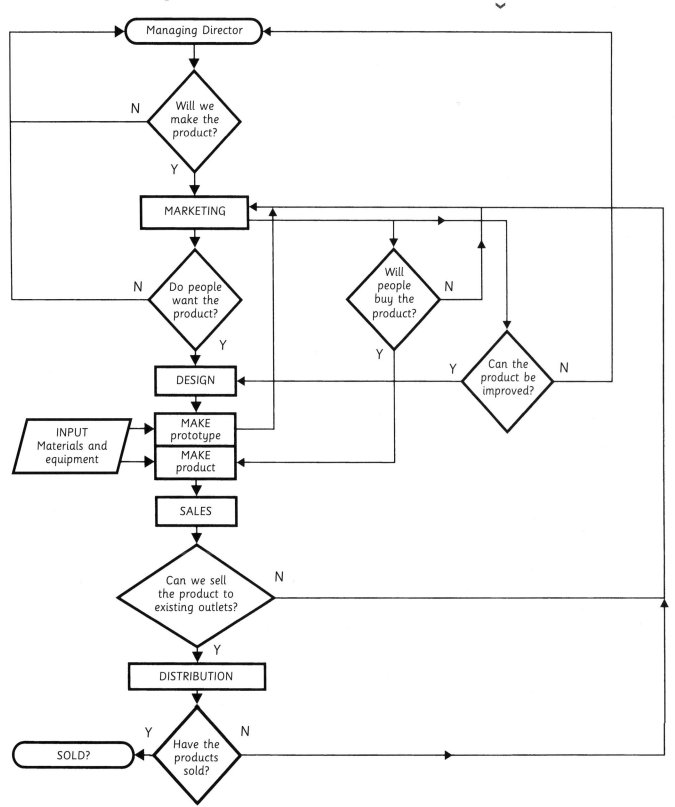

The importance of good organisation and systematic working in the manufacture of textile goods

Many of the decisions mean that the product design has to return to an earlier stage. For example, if market research using the prototype suggests that improvements should be made to the design, the designer will have to redesign the product to take account of this finding. This ensures that the final product is as good as it can be.

When you are making your product, you will be responsible for all the stages. You have to take extra care that you do not miss any stages. You must work in the most organised way possible to ensure a successful result, completed on time and within your budget.

Subsystems

Each department shown in the flowchart will be organised as a subsystem or a set of subsystems which each have a beginning and an end.

Maximising efficiency

A system should run smoothly if it is to be efficient.

> Work is organised so that as few people as possible are waiting for something to do.

> Careful planning ensures that expensive equipment is not lying idle.

> Checks must be kept in place to make sure that work is completed to a high standard before moving to the next stage. This is **quality assurance**.

Job descriptions

Each person in the organisation has a job description so that they know exactly what they should be doing. There must be someone in each section who has the knowledge and understanding to ensure that a job is complete before moving to the next stage.

Types of production systems

One-off

This is where only one product of a particular design is made. This type of production includes the items that you make yourself for your own satisfaction. Normally, the originals of fashionable clothing and prototypes of other textile goods will begin as a single example and be shown to a selected audience by members of the marketing department.

Batch production

Most textile goods are produced in batches. Once a prototype design has been selected for production, a small batch will be made and offered for sale in selected **retail outlets**. If the sale of the goods is successful, the manufacturer will go into mass production. Textile goods which are made in different colours and different sizes and are dependent on changes in fashion are normally produced in batches.

Mass production

The most efficient type of industrial production is continuous production where the product flows through all the processes needed, as smoothly as possible, without the manufacturer having to make any changes. The production line will be operational for 24 hours a day, 7 days a week. Continuous production is normal in the spinning and weaving industry, and for making textile goods such as nappies, which are not sensitive to changes in fashion.

Case studies

This section shows how two products – a waistcoat and a cushion cover – can be made. You should be able to make these two products, as well as gain ideas for your own products.

Waistcoat

Many people have to buy items of mass-produced clothing which can be worn for many different occasions. A waistcoat can be an economical way of changing an ordinary outfit into a very individual and interesting one for a particular occasion. This case study shows you how you could make a waistcoat.

The design considerations are shown below, with comments.

Design consideration	Comment
The purpose or occasion for which the waistcoat is being made.	A smart waistcoat for special occasions such as parties or discos.
The limit on the budget. However attractive the product may be, the costs must be kept within the agreed limit.	As it can be used to 'liven up' an everyday outfit, the client may be able to consider something that is a little bit extravagant.
Pattern making: will the pattern be purchased, or will you make your own?	Decide on a particular style and buy a paper pattern.
The availability of all the suitable fabrics and other items.	Brainstorming needed here.
The time that is available. Customers will not be very pleased with a rushed job, but a sensible completion date must be agreed.	Make a careful plan of time needed for making. Allow for access to equipment, which may be restricted.
Available equipment. The fact that you sometimes use a particular piece of equipment does not mean that it will always be available to you; some tasks will be given priority over others. In textiles classes, priority is given to the student whose design has been most thoroughly prepared.	Check that the equipment is reliable and available. You may find that some machines are more popular than others, and will have to consider this.

Buy a paper pattern. There is often a choice of patterns which include shirts and trousers with the waistcoat, and others that offer up to nine waistcoat designs in one easy pattern. Here are the most common styles.

Before making your fabric choice, remember:

> If handwoven fabric is to be used, it must be woven on a loom at least 300 mm wide.

> Knitted fabric must be made to exactly the same size as the pattern piece and must be bonded with an interfacing to give it stability.

> Plain fabric can be decorated using any of the techniques described in Chapter 3.

> You could select a finished fabric from a wide range.

> Consider the colour, tone, line, texture and pattern of the fabric.

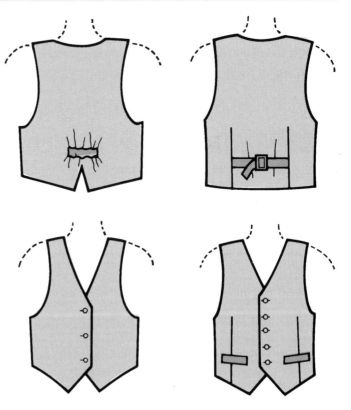

Waistcoat styles. >

There is often a difference between the fabric used for the front and that used for the back of a waistcoat. If more than one item is being made, this is more economical than using the same fabric for front and back – the more expensive material is used for the front.

This method may not be economical for a one-off design. The pattern piece must be laid with the grainline or warp threads of the fabric going down the garment, rather than across it. For example, look at the layout shown here. When you have cut out the fronts, you may have sufficient left for the back, or to make a matching cravat or tie.

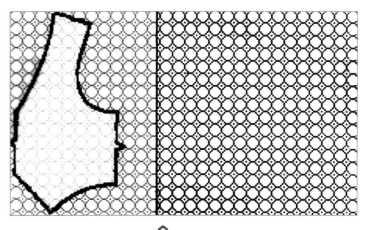

Pattern layout for a waistcoat.

An individually-decorated waistcoat will take time, and this effort is reduced if only the front is decorated. Time and effort can be very costly and add to the client's bill.

A piece of satin is traditionally used for the back. Again, there will be a large piece left over and you can consider using the same fabric for the back as for the lining. You need to look at the layouts to see if any cost savings can be made.

You will need buttons and probably a buckle. Covered buttons give a reliable match but can be difficult to make with fabrics that are bulky or that fray easily. It is very important to think about the buttons *before* buying the fabric – there is no point in spending a lot of money if your design is 'let down' by buttons that are not quite right.

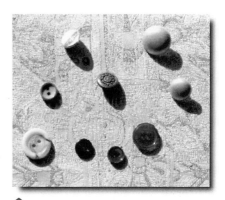

A piece of fabric with a choice of buttons.

The client's measurements must be checked and the paper pattern can be altered as necessary. There are clear directions given on the pattern pieces for making alterations. (A fashion designer would make a **toile**, or mock-up, of the garment in order to check that the style is right.) You should cut out the lining first and stitch the shoulder and side seams together using a long machine stitch that can be easily removed. The client can try this on to check that the garment will fit. When you are sure that the fitting is correct, remove the stitching from the seams and sew the shoulder seams with a stitch of a suitable length.

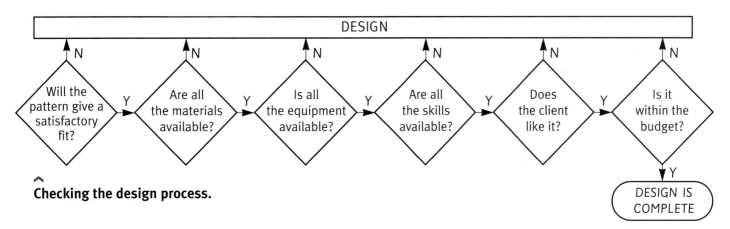

Checking the design process.

Making the waistcoat

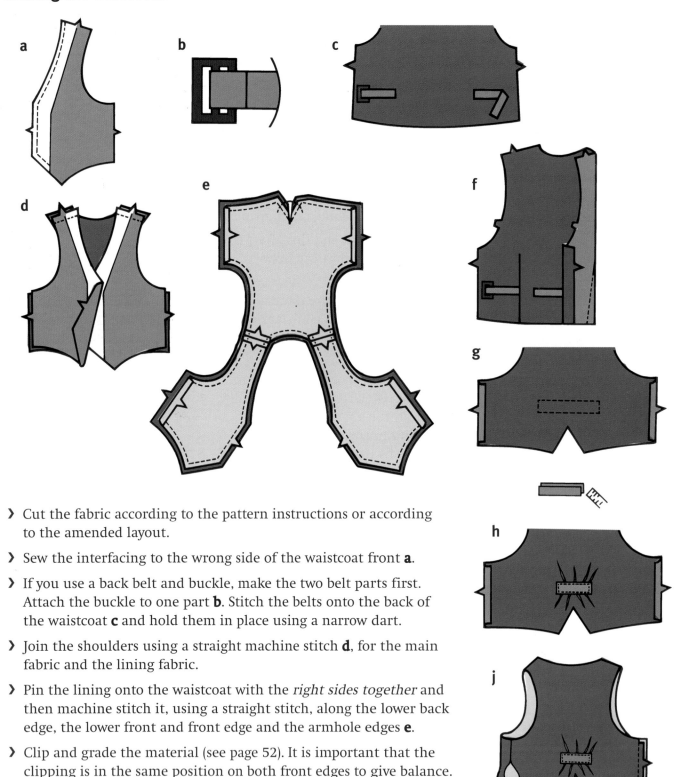

> Cut the fabric according to the pattern instructions or according to the amended layout.

> Sew the interfacing to the wrong side of the waistcoat front **a**.

> If you use a back belt and buckle, make the two belt parts first. Attach the buckle to one part **b**. Stitch the belts onto the back of the waistcoat **c** and hold them in place using a narrow dart.

> Join the shoulders using a straight machine stitch **d**, for the main fabric and the lining fabric.

> Pin the lining onto the waistcoat with the *right sides together* and then machine stitch it, using a straight stitch, along the lower back edge, the lower front and front edge and the armhole edges **e**.

> Clip and grade the material (see page 52). It is important that the clipping is in the same position on both front edges to give balance. Although the line at the bottom may appear smooth, minor differences in clipping may make the two curves appear different. *The side seams must not be stitched at this stage.*

> Turn out to the right side using a gap in the side seam, and press it carefully.

> If you are using an elastic casing on the back, machine stitch along the casing lines **g** and insert a piece of elastic 2 cm wide and 16 cm long. You can attach a safety pin to the elastic so that it can be pulled through more easily.

> Stitch the casing firmly at each end **h**. It is possible to do this with a decorative machine stitch if there is a suitable one available.

> Hand sew the side seams of the lining together with a slip-stitch. (If this garment was to be mass-produced you would join together both layers of the fabric for the side seams by machine.)

You may wish to change the position of a pocket to suit the fabric pattern, as in the case of this strip patchwork waistcoat.

Buttons and buttonholes are best left until last, and the position of these must be carefully checked. One of the buttons must be at or just above the waistline. If a button is just below the waistline with a large gap above it, the wearer will have a rather 'droopy' appearance.

The result is a very individual garment, finished to a high standard.

Positioning a pocket on a strip patchwork waistcoat.

Cushion cover

The design considerations for this are similar to those shown on page 76 for the waistcoat, except you should make your own pattern. Begin by looking at existing products.

The front of the cover is cut to the same size as the cushion to be covered plus 30 mm to allow for seams. The back of the cover is cut to this width plus 50 mm to allow for the opening. This piece is then cut along the line where the client wishes to have the opening. The client may wish to have one of the following finishes:

> a frill of the same fabric,

> a frill of contrasting fabric,

> a piped border,

> a lace border.

The amount of material needs to be carefully calculated before beginning production. The position and type of fastenings should be the client's choice.

Making the cushion cover

> The openings and fastenings are worked first.

Zipper opening
Tack the edges of the opening together and press the seam open. The zipper is sewn into place as shown on page 53.

Flap opening
Fold over the edges of the opening and hem them. Press-fasteners of any type can be sewn onto the hemmed area or a suitable weight of Velcro fastening can be used.

> If the front panel of the cushion is to be decorated, you should complete this before the cushion is made up.

> The back should be fastened and treated as one piece of fabric.

> Piping or frills should be sewn in place as shown here.

The two sides are placed with right sides facing and stitched together. Great care must be taken to ensure that frills are not caught up in the stitching.

> A three-thread flatlock stitch on an overlocker can give a decorative edge on some cushions. In this case the two parts of the cushion are laid with the reverse (wrong) sides together. Thread is chosen to enhance the cushion.

All the stages of the process must be clearly planned and a checklist written down before actually making the cushion. If the design and planning is efficiently completed, the cushion cover can then be made.

Evaluating the outcomes

You should evaluate the process for designing and making these products at each stage and record them in your journal. You should make a full evaluation of the finished product.

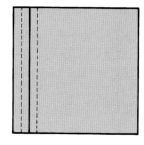

Zipper opening

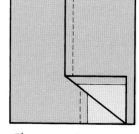

Flap opening

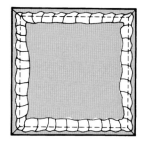

Sewing the cushion with a frill

^
Sewing piping or frills in place.

There is a wide range of threads, in many colours and qualities, for use in decorating textile products.
⌄

Summary

You should now know:
> about systems,
> the importance of good organisation and systematic working when manufacturing textile goods,
> about different types of production systems,
> how to make two textile items – a waistcoat and a cushion cover.

Activities

1 Draw a flowchart for one subsystem such as designing or making a garment of your choice.

2 Write job descriptions for two people who would be employed in the industrial production of *either* a garment *or* a cushion cover.

3 Make a checklist of *all* the points you would make to check that one of the products described in this chapter is finished. For example, is the waistcoat finished if you can pull a loose end and a button falls off?

4 Look at a book on pattern making and make a pattern for a garment of your choice, or use a pattern-making application on a computer system to make a pattern. Evaluate the results.

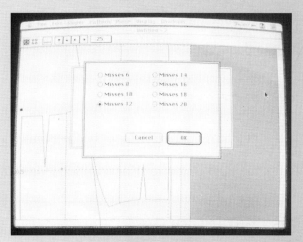

'Fittingly sew' package screen.

5 Make one of the products described in this chapter.

Questions

1 Match the following with the correct flowchart box.
   a Fabric and thread.
   b Begin.
   c Is the prototype satisfactory?
   d Binding a cushion.

A   B

C   D

Flowchart boxes.

2 Draw a diagram to show a system for the process of cutting bias strips.

3 Why are fashion goods normally produced in batches rather than as one-off items?

4 Which of these textile products could be made by continuous production methods:
   › sweatshirts
   › babies' nappies
   › surgical dressings
   › trousers
   › panties?
   Give reasons for your answers.

5 Why would a manufacturer avoid the use of hand sewing in the manufacture of textile goods?

6 When buying a waistcoat pattern you are presented with two choices:
   a several styles of waistcoat in one packet,
   b patterns for trousers and a shirt in the same packet.
   Which would you choose and why?

7 There is a wide choice of fastenings for the cushion. Say which you would choose for mass production, giving reasons for your choice.

9 Selling

For a design to be commercially successful, a marketing strategy needs to be used to encourage people to buy the product. Many different marketing strategies have been developed.

This chapter focuses on:

› advertising,

› packaging,

› displaying goods.

Advertising

Advertising is how people are attracted to a product and is the main link between the manufacturer and the consumer. The manufacturer puts forward an image of the product which is intended to appeal to a target market. For example, fashion models may be used by clothing manufacturers to advertise the latest range.

There are many methods of advertising, including:

› television,　› radio,

› newspapers,　› magazines,

› Internet,　› cinemas,

› billboards,

› transport, for example buses and Underground trains.

Some examples of advertising.

Different methods or media are employed to attract a different audience. For example, a product aimed at young people is unlikely to be advertised on television late at night, but is likely to be advertised in magazines for young people. The theme will also be different for different target groups. For example, an advertisement for young people may be based around the latest craze, or may feature a pop star.

Advertisements are designed to persuade people to buy the goods. They use images and personality types that are likely to appeal to the people whom they target. Fashion items can be presented using very emotive images such as sex appeal. People who engage in sport have successful sports personalities as their role models. Advertising will take advantage of this but will also give factual information about the performance of the products. Furnishings are presented in the homes of people who are – or who appear to be – wealthy and successful. Even products which the rich and famous would be unlikely to buy are presented in this way to make people believe that they are buying a luxurious product at a modest price.

Designing advertising

You can design the advertising for your own textiles products. You will find that a computer is helpful for this. You can word-process the text, and then combine it with graphics that you have produced by hand, or using a graphics program to produce a well-presented advertisement.

Packaging

Packages take many different forms. The form of the packaging for a product will depend on the product being sold (for example, food products require different packaging from textile items) and the image the seller wishes to project (for example, a product aimed at the luxury market may be wrapped in fine tissue packaging, whereas a product at the other end of the range may not be wrapped at all). Packaging has four main functions.

1 To protect the product.

2 To provide information about the product.

3 To promote the product.

4 To preserve the product.

In fact, packaging will probably fulfil more than one of these functions for a product. For example, a plastic clothes cover may protect the garment, have printed information about the garment and its manufacturer, and have printed promotional material about the garment.

Packaging can protect the product.

Packaging can provide information about the product.

The Trade Descriptions Act exists to make sure that the information that is given in advertisements and on packaging is correct and does not mislead the customer. Misleading information may be given unintentionally, so standards are produced by the British Standards Institution to ensure that information about the content of the product and its care is quite clear.

If things go wrong, the customer can complain to the local Trading Standards Officer who can enforce the laws. It would be sensible for you to seek advice from your local Trading Standards Officer to avoid making mistakes if you want to market your product.

Packaging can promote the product.

Designing packaging

There are various approaches that you can use to design the packaging for your product. A good starting point would be to look at existing packaging to see how its design could be modified to suit your needs. You could use a CAD program to design nets for packaging and trial various options before making the final decision.

Ties
by Ralph

You will need to consider the surface decoration for the packaging. You could use various graphical techniques and media for this, including coloured pencils, marker pens, paints, stencils and collage. You will need to take into account the information about labelling for textile products given on page 37.

This net for packaging has a window for viewing the goods.

Displaying goods

The way in which goods are displayed affects sales. If customers cannot see the products properly, they are less likely to buy them. Shops give a lot of attention to window-dressing because an eye-catching display can draw customers into a shop, where they may buy more than one item. Within shops, the position of goods is important. The layout of large supermarkets is planned carefully to maximise sales. Department stores group articles of clothing together, by design and then by colour. The aim is to tempt a customer to buy more than one item at a time. For example, you may go to buy a skirt or a pair of trousers, but see a blouse or shirt that matches it nearby, and buy both.

Clothes displayed in a department store.

A room display for soft furnishings.

When you display your textiles items, for whatever purpose, you should make sure that you have arranged them attractively. If necessary, you should iron them before displaying them so that they look as good as possible. You may be able to change the lighting conditions around your items to show any sheen on the fabrics that you have used.

Summary

You should now know about:

> advertising,

> packaging,

> displaying textile items.

Activities

1 Select a product and collect advertisements for it. Also collect a sample of its package. Discuss some of the marketing techniques used, for example factual, emotive, sex appeal and status. Analyse these advertisements in terms of the images they are creating for the product.

2 Develop a logo for a textiles company of your choice. It should clearly reflect the image of the company. It should look good on small objects and also on the side of transport vehicles.

3 See what you can find out about the history of packaging. Select a product or type of product and research its package development over the last 20 years.

4 Collect four advertisements from a magazine or newspaper and answer the following questions.
   ❯ What type of advertisement is it (is it emotive, factual, etc.)?
   ❯ Who is it aimed at?
   ❯ Is it convincing?
   ❯ Is it appealing?
   ❯ How is it trying to persuade you to buy the product?

5 Design a suitable package for a tie, a cravat or tie-backs.

6 Imagine that you are setting up in business making either clothes or soft furnishings. You have a very small shop window. Draw a sketch to show how you would make the best use of the window for displaying your products.

Questions

1 Give the names of six different places where firms advertise goods.

2 Give four reasons for using packaging.

3 How does the way in which goods are displayed encourage people to spend more money?

4 Why are successful sports personalities used to advertise sportswear?

5 What is the name of the officer who is employed by the local authority to ensure that legal trading standards are maintained?

6 How would you make sure that your goods were correctly described?

10 Back to the future

The development of textiles has been influenced by a variety of factors, but in particular by technology.

This final chapter focuses on:

> influences of technology on the textile industry in the past,

> influences of changes in technology on textile products,

> environmental issues relating to textiles products,

> uses of textiles.

Influences of technology on the textile industry in the past

Fabric production

In 1733, John Kay introduced a new invention which led to huge advances in the weaving industry. It was called the *flying shuttle*, and it meant that weaving was much faster, easier and more versatile, because only one hand was required to throw the shuttle back and forth. This put pressure on the spinning industry to produce yarn more quickly to match the faster rate of weaving.

In 1763, James Hargreaves invented the *spinning jenny*. This was followed by Richard Arkwright's *water-frame spinning machine* in 1769, and Samuel Crompton's *spinning mule* in 1779, which combined characteristics of the spinning jenny and spinning machine. All of these machines led to vast improvements in the industry.

**James Hargreaves'
spinning jenny.**

Dr Edmund Cartwright patented his first power-driven loom in 1785 and a newer version in 1787. This gave the factories even greater output.

^ A Jacquard loom.

^ A modern computer-controlled loom.

In 1732, one of the biggest advances in weaving took place in the French silk industry when J. M. Jacquard invented a loom that could automatically weave patterns. This was the first loom to produce tapestry-like textiles mechanically using punched cards. A whole new area of textiles was developed. The punched card was really a digital information-processing medium similar to that used in a computer.

Developments were also made in carding. In 1748 David Bourn and Lewis Paul patented a carding machine that could separate cotton or short fibres of wool. By 1785, Arkwright had developed a machine which could card continuously.

Perhaps the most notable advances in spinning came around 1850, when G. E. Donisthorpe introduced the ring spindle. This spindle rotated at high speed and produced yarn much more rapidly. It significantly improved the quality of worsted yarn.

All of these inventions led to a textiles industry that could produce far greater quantities of fabric in less time. Computers are now a part of all stages of the process, from the initial development of the raw materials through to designing, production and marketing of the end product.

Sewing machines

In 1851, Isaac Singer produced the first commercially-available sewing machine which became very popular because it saved so much time, and the number sold grew rapidly. The first sewing machines were hand operated and only sewed forward. Now there are many different types of sewing machine, which allow you to produce complex, quality products. Computer-operated sewing machines can do complex operations such as embroidery, monograms and circular buttonholes.

Isaac Singer's first sewing machine
built in 1851.

A modern sewing machine
linked to a computer.

Knitting machines

Knitting is one of the simplest and cheapest ways for people to make
fabric from yarn. Using two or four knitting needles, it is possible to
produce a wide variety of items and patterns.

William Lee invented the first knitting machine in 1589. He called
it the 'stocking frame'. It was used to knit stockings in plain knitting.
In the mid-eighteenth century the design
was altered so that it was also possible
to knit ribbed stockings. In the
mid-nineteenth century there were
rapid advances in home and industrial
knitting machines.

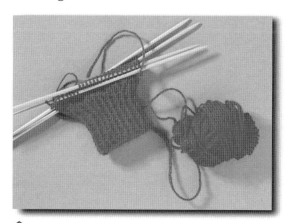

Hand knitting.

A modern computerised ❯
knitting machine.

Influences of changes in technology on textile products

Clothing

Clothing changes as new fabrics and processes become available. In the past, only the rich were able to be fashionable.

Now, due to cheaper fabrics, more people are able to keep up with fashions if they wish to. The introduction of synthetic fibres has led to vast changes in the properties of fabrics. There are many different styles of clothing now. And nearly anything is acceptable!

^
The development of clothing.

❬ Different styles of clothing in the 1990s.

Fashion is very competitive. A huge international industry has developed. There are large numbers of people associated with the industry, from the production of the fibre to the sale of the finished goods.

Workwear

There are some jobs, for example nursing and police work, in which the workers have uniforms that must be worn for safety, health and identity. Members of the armed forces, police and security guards require special protective clothing that will not impede movement. The highest performance that can be gained without restricting the wearer's movement will continue to be an important area for research and development. There are also jobs which, although they don't have a set uniform, still call for a certain type of dress. (For example, a motor mechanic wears tough overalls, while a shop assistant may need to look neat and tidy.)

Textiles in the home

Washing machines have made it easier to wash curtains, chair coverings and other textile items. The fabrics themselves have become easier to care for. Home furnishings are now lighter and brighter-looking than in the past.

Technical textiles

Technical textiles are 'textile products manufactured for their performance characteristics and are used in industry, institutional, civil engineering, medical or leisure applications' (Commission of the European Communities, 1991). In 1995, about 25 per cent of textiles in Europe and 40 per cent in Japan were used for technical purposes and the proportion seems likely to increase.

Textiles in industry

The increased use of dangerous chemicals has resulted in a need for highly specialised protective clothing. Increased concerns about personal safety have added to this demand. The increase in mass production involves the increased use of textiles in items such as conveyor belts.

Textiles in leisure goods

Much of the increased leisure time that people have is spent on travel. Making lighter-weight, less bulky luggage is very important as many retired people spend an increased amount of time on holiday travel. Comfort and safety needs, which are continually changing, make special demands on textile designers. In 1980, air bags in cars were uncommon but most cars built in 1995 were fitted with them.

There have been huge changes in the types of clothing worn for sport. For example, bathers wore neck-to-knee garments in the 1930s! Synthetic materials now allow the manufacture of sportswear that is quick and easy to wash and dry, stretches, is brightly coloured and light to wear. These bright, comfortable fabrics are used for aerobics, gymnastics and similar activities.

Reducing bulk in garments which keep people warm has made ski suits much more attractive. It is now possible to reinforce knee and elbow areas without having unwanted bulkiness.

Wetsuits can now be made that are more pliable than they used to be. This means that watersports now have a much wider appeal.

Textiles are used in tennis balls, tennis and badminton racquets, watersports equipment, synthetic turf and artificial ski slopes, and in many other items.

Textiles and medical applications

Textiles are widely used in hospitals and medical centres. Soluble yarn is used in some circumstances where stitches would be awkward to remove. Fabrics that are not attacked by micro-organisms can be used to give support to internal organs during surgery. Textiles are used for filters in hospital equipment. Fewer textiles are used for dressing wounds than before 1960.

Textiles in agriculture and horticulture

Farmers and market gardeners have used sacks, twine and nettings for centuries but many new fibres have been introduced in the latter part of the twentieth century. For example, when you buy a cucumber from a supermarket, it will probably have been grown on rockwool. The risk of infection to plants in glasshouses is greatly reduced if rockwool is used rather than soil. In the past, soil was disinfected with substances that created health hazards for the growers.

The use of mats rather than straw for cattle kept inside has resulted in a much higher standard of hygiene, although this has created the problem of what to use the straw for now.

Large areas of plants are grown in rockwool.

Textiles in construction and civil engineering

From earliest times, many people have lived in tents. Tents are often considered to be temporary structures used for camping, village fêtes or the circus. Large tent structures have been developed for more permanent buildings, such as the Pavilion in Llangollen shown on page 29.

Environmental issues relating to textiles

When you are designing, you must take environmental issues into account.

Recycling

Fabric goods are normally recycled quite efficiently. When an eighteenth-century couple had their clothes made, the dressmaker or tailor would be a man (women worked only as seamstresses) who came to their house. They would trade-in their old clothes and the dressmaker would sell them on, just as motor cars are traded today. By the time the clothes reached the poorest people they were worn to shreds and rapidly degraded, wherever they were dumped. Today, clothing is likely to be sent to a jumble sale or charity shop and when it is outworn, it may be collected by a recycling service. Rugs and other items can be made from the waste fibres from textile production.

Proteinic and cellulosic fibres are just plant and animal materials and so do not normally present a problem. If they are dumped in hedgerows they are unsightly and offensive but they do not present a serious threat.

Non-cellulosic fibres take longer to degrade and some are designed to be rot-proof. The main environmental problems occur during the various production processes. For example, when rayon is made, sodium hydroxide and carbon disulphide are used to break down the cellulose fibres to form a pulp. Sodium hydroxide is the very caustic chemical that is used in some oven cleaners and has to be neutralised using an acid, before it can be disposed of as a waste product. New laws have restricted the amount of such waste that can be allowed to pollute the environment. Specialist fibres, such as those from hospitals which must be burnt, present a particular problem.

An important development is Tencel, which is made by Courtaulds using a new solvent for making the pulp. As much as 99 per cent of this solvent can be reclaimed. Tencel can be spun and woven to meet a wide range of specifications, from rough denim to fine, soft velvet. This suggests the direction for further research.

'Golden hamstrings': textile product made from recycled cotton, nylon, wool, acrylic, jersey, lycra, crimplene.

The consequences of new design

When you design new products you change things that already exist. Many of the changes you make are of little lasting consequence but some can have a considerable influence on people's lives. You must consider the consequences of any changes you make so that what you do is of benefit to yourself and to your clients without harming others.

Uses of technical textiles

The table below summarises the most important uses of technical textiles.

Market areas	Products/Applications
Automotive industry	Seats, seat covers, seatbelts, air bags, carpets, flexible and fabric roofs, tyre card and tyre textiles, air and oil filters, body reinforcement, transmission belts, etc.
Civil engineering Geotextiles for rail, road	Textiles for railway track, road, dam and embankment reinforcement, stabilisation, drainage, soil erosion protection, river banks, etc.
Buildings and structures	'Air houses', temporary buildings, marquees, concrete reinforcement, sound insulation, vibration damping, etc.
Coated	Tarpaulins, aircraft escape chutes, inflatable boats, flexible hoses, flexible fuel and water tanks etc. used extensively in civil engineering, medicine, protective textiles and textiles for sport and leisure
Horticulture and agriculture	Rockwool for plant cultures, agricultural harvest and horticultural twine, wind screens and fencings, moisture-retention layers for soil, water transmission fabrics, tarpaulins, nettings, agricultural bags, cattle mats, etc.
Industrial	Filters and filtration materials, applications (gas filters, liquid/solid filters, cigarette filters, etc.), conveyor belts, hoses, power transmission belts, fishing nets, battery separators, dielectric fabrics, insulating fabrics, optical fibres, cable covers and binding, papermakers' felts, etc.
Medical	Bandages, gauzes, lints, surgical gowns, face masks, gloves, surgical sutures, hospital uniforms, sanitary products, stretchers, artificial limbs, ligaments, cardiac patches, dialysis and filter units, etc.
Protective	Boiler suits, overalls, thermally resistant workwear, racing drivers'/astronauts' suits, waterproof outerwear, fire protective wear, bullet-proof vests, gas masks, diving suits, awnings, parachute fabric and harness
Sports and leisure	Synthetic turf, golf club shafts, billiard table cloths, sail cloth, tennis/squash etc. racquets/strings, hockey sticks, fishing rods and lines, ball game nets, boat/canoe/yacht body panel reinforcement, linings/covers for pool/boat etc., survival clothing for cold-weather expeditions, climbing ropes, musical instrument strings and body panels, flexible dinghies, bouncy castles, artificial ski slopes, etc.
Miscellaneous	Fibre/textile reinforced composites for aircraft, machinery and various other high-performance components, industrial sewing threads, fibrous insulation, paint brushes, laundry bags, wigs, etc.

Summary

You should now know:

> something about the influences of technology on the textile industry in the past,

> something about influences of changes in technology on textiles products,

> about environmental issues relating to textiles,

> about some uses of textiles.

Activities

1 Conduct a survey of the sewing machines or knitting machines owned by the families of members of your class. What age is each machine and what tasks does it perform? How often is it used? What do the people using it make? You may wish to find out how the use of the machine has changed over the years.

2 Select one invention mentioned in this chapter and find out more about it. Why did it come about? What influences did it have on the industry?

3 There are textile manufacturers throughout Britain. Select one in your region and try to find out something about its history.

4 The Seminole Indians were some of the first people to use Singer's new invention. They tore calico into strips and machined these in a variety of ways to make patchwork garments. Go to your library and look at patchwork patterns. Choose one that can be made by machine and one that must be worked by hand, and make drawings of these.

5 Select a sport that interests you. Obtain a photograph or make a drawing of the clothes that would normally be worn by people learning the sport. Do the same for a champion performer. Describe the similarities and differences. What influences changes in the design of sportswear?

6 There are many collection points for recycling or reusing textile goods. Find out what collections there are in your area. Could this be improved?

7 What happens to your garments and soft furnishings when you have finished with them? Are you disposing of them in a responsible way?

8 Make a list of ways for extending the life of garments that you have tired of.

9 For this activity you will need a plastic bag of the type given free at some shops. Cut the top off it. With the bag open, cut a narrow strip so that you continue to cut it in a spiral. By the time you reach the base of the bag you will have a length of 'yarn' which can be used for knitting, weaving, crochet or braiding. You will find that it is quite similar to 'plastic raffia'. Think of a possible use for it. What are the practical problems of using this to produce goods?

Questions

1 What was the name of John Kay's invention? When did he invent it?

2 Who invented the spinning jenny? When was it invented?

3 When was the first power-driven loom patented?

4 What was the name of the Frenchman who invented a loom that could weave patterns automatically?

5 Who invented a machine that could card fibre continuously?

6 Who invented the first commercially-available sewing machine?

7 What effect did the inventions mentioned in this chapter have on the textile industry?

8 What are the advantages of a modern computerised sewing machine compared with a nineteenth-century sewing machine?

9 Name two depleted natural resources.

10 Name two types of pollution.

11 What is a renewable resource?

12 To what extent are the resources used in the manufacture of cellulosic fabrics renewable?

Glossary

anthropometrics
The measurement of the human body and its proportions.

bark cloth
A traditional fabric made in South America, Africa and Polynesia from the bark of trees belonging to the mulberry family.

blended
Fibres of a different colour, quality or source are mixed together to give a uniform quality.

blends
The name given to fabrics that are produced from blended fibres.

cellulose
Constituent of the cell walls of plants. Used to make rayon and some plastics.

crêpe
A thin silk-like cloth with a wrinkled surface.

dupion
A type of woven silk fabric containing thicker areas of yarn (slubs).

dye-fastness
The measurement of a dye's ability to retain its colour over time.

ergonomics
The study of the relationship between people and their working environment.

felt
A non-woven fabric made by matting and compressing hairs.

fibre
A single strand of hair from a sheep's back or a single strand from a cotton boll. Synthetic fibres are sometimes referred to as filaments.

filament
A long continuous fibre such as that produced by a silkworm or by synthetic fibre production.

flannel
A soft, loosely woven material, originally made in woollen or worsted, but also made from brushed cotton.

floats
Long, loose warp yarns lying on the right side of fabric – usually satin, silk or rayon. They catch the light and give the fabric a characteristic shine.

ginning
The process that removes the seeds from cotton lint.

integrated package
A software package for a microcomputer system that contains a wordprocessor, spreadsheet, database and graphics applications. The integration makes it possible to switch from one part to another, and to transfer information between the parts.

jute
A strong fibre obtained from the jute plant.

linker
A machine that is used to join the seams of knitwear by making a series of loops.

lint
The ball of cottonwool produced by the cotton plant.

milling
A finishing process in which fabric is brushed to raise the fibre ends.

nylon
A synthetic plastic material used to make fabric.

plain
The simplest weave, where the weft passes over one thread and under one thread, with an even number of warp threads. In knitting, plain knitting is the same as that achieved when hand-knitting a row of plain (knit) stitches alternating with a row of purl stitches.

polyamide
A particular group of synthetic materials, of which nylon is one.

polyester
A synthetic resin/fibre used to make fabric.

polymerisation
The process of joining together molecules to form polymers.

proteinic fibres
Fibres produced by animals and made from proteins.

purl
A type of knitting that combines knit and rib stitches.

quality assurance
A system of checks to ensure that work is completed to a high standard before it moves onto the next stage.

rayon
The first synthetic fibre. Rayon is made from cellulose.

reeling
The process of unwinding a silkworm cocoon and putting the filament onto a reel.

retail outlets
Places where manufactured goods are sold to individual customers.

retting
A process for removing the strong fibres from a plant.

reverse
The back or less important side of a textile or textile product.

rib
An edge formed by knitting plain and purl stitches to give a very elastic fabric.

roving
Yarn that has not been spun.

sliver
Strands of fibre that are not yet formed into yarn.

slubs
Thick areas of yarn which show as a thicker line in woven fabrics. They are characteristic of linen and silk dupion.

spinnerets
The tiny holes through which a substance is extruded to form a filament.

spinning
The twisting together of many fibres or filaments to form a continuous thread or yarn.

staple
A grade of fibre which is measured of finite length – not a filament.

toile
A garment made from calico which is used to obtain a fit before cutting out the garment from a more expensive fabric.

tweed
A hard-wearing patterned woollen cloth woven from yarns of different colours.

Vilene®
A particular brand of non-woven fabric that is used to support and add body to fabrics (used in collars, cuffs, waistbands, etc.).

viscose
Fabric made from a viscous solution of cellulose.

wad
Any mass of fibres which has not been made into yarn or fabric.

wadding
Layers of fibres that are used for padding, stuffing or quilting.

warp knitting
A row of loops formed vertically using a number of threads, each controlled by its own needle.

waxing
The process of coating a garment with wax to make it waterproof.

weaving
The technique of making fabric by interlacing two sets of threads (warp and weft) at right-angles.

weft knitting
A single yarn runs horizontally making a row of loops into which the following row of loops are knitted.

woollen system
Process of making fabrics from shorter woollen fibres, usually blankets and knitted items.

worsted
Fabric made from long-staple fibres of the same length tightly twisted to give a smooth surface.

Index

absorbency 35
acoustic properties (fabrics) 35
acrylic fibres, blends 11
advertising 82ñ3
aesthetics 35, 61
agricultural uses of textiles 92
animal fibres 5ñ6
anthropometrics 61
appliquÈ 27
asbestos fibres 6

bark cloth 18
batch production 75
batik 24
beads 27
belts 55
binding (edges) 53
blended fibres 10ñ11
blind hem 52
Bondaweb 27
bonded fabrics 22
braids and trims 53
brainstorming 62
British Standards 36, 84
brushed fabrics 28
buckles 55
burning test 33ñ4
buttons 54, 77

carding 11, 12, 88
care labels 37, 44
carpet weaving 18
cashmere 6
cellulosic fibres 4, 7, 93
clothing, development 90ñ91
coated fabrics 29
colour 59-60
combing 11, 12
comfort properties (fabrics) 35
computer-aided design (CAD) 69, 84
computer-aided manufacture 55

computers
    database compilation 3
    information presentation 43
    linked to sewing machine 26, 55,
        88, 89
    preparation of advertisement 83
    preparation of drawings 68-9
    preparation of questionnaire 42
construction techniques 49ñ53
consumer choice, factors in 44
Consumer Protection Act 37
consumer rights 37
cotton 4, 10, 11
    blends 11
creasing tests 34
crêpe 16
cushion cover, production 79-80
cutting out 55

databases
    fabrics 19
    fibres 3
degradability (fabrics) 28
design 57-70
design analysis 40
design brief 64-5
design plan 66ñ7
disassembling 46, 64
discharge printing 24
displaying goods 85
drawing (yarn) 11, 12
drawings 67, 68
dupion 13
dyefastness 23
dyeing 22-4

efficiency of systems 74
embroidery 26
environmental issues 93
ergonomics 61
evaluation of product 80

fabric painting 25
fabrics 1
    database 19
    properties 31-5
fashion 90-91
fastenings 53-5
felt 18
fibres 1
    database 3
    natural 4-6
    processing 10-14
    synthetic 7-8, 14
filaments 10
    continuous 14
flame-retardant finishes 28, 36
flammability tests 31, 36
flannel 16
flat seam 49
flax 4
floats 15
flowcharts 40, 72-3
French seam 50
function analysis 63
Funtex 27

gilling 12
ginning 4, 11
glitter fabrics 29
GoretexÆ 22
graphical techniques 43, 68

hems and edges 52-3
home furnishings 91

insulation properties (fabrics) 35

Jacquard loom 88
job descriptions 74
jute 18

knitted fabrics 17–18, 48
knitting machines 89

labelling 37, 44
lace making 19
laminated fabrics 22
leather 19, 47
  simulated 18, 22
legislation 36–7
leisure goods 91–2
line (design element) 58
linen 4
linkers 48
lint 4

machine embroidery 26, 27
machine sewing 47–8, 88–9
mass production 75
medical uses of textiles 92
milling 16
mineral fibres 6, 92
mockups 70, 77

natural fibres 4–6
needles 46–7
noil spinning 13, 14
non-cellulosic fibres 7–8
nylon 7–8

one-off production 75
overlockers 48

packaging 83ñ4
patchwork quilts 22
pattern 60
piped seams 51
plain knitting 17
plain weave 15
plant fibres 4
polyamide 8
polycotton 11
polyester 8
  blends 11
polymerisation 7
presenting information 42–3
press fasteners 55
pressing 53
printing 24
production systems 75
protective clothing 91
proteinic fibres 5, 93
purl knitting 17

quality assurance 74
questionnaires 42
quilting 21–2

random dyeing 23
rayon 7, 93
recording and reporting (test
    results) 32–3
recycling of textiles 93
reeling (silk) 14
rendering 68
research 39–42
retail outlets 75
retting 4
rib knitting 17
roller printing 24
roving 12

Safety at Work Act 36
samples 69
satin weave 15
scissors 49
seam and fell 50
seams 49–52
selling 82–5
sequins 27
sewing machines 26, 55, 88–9
shape (design element) 59
shot silk 16
shrinkage 35
silica fibres 6
silk 6
    database card 3
    yarn 13ñ14
silk screen printing 24
sliver 12
slubs 12
soft toys 36
specification 66
spinnerets 7, 14
spinning 11, 12, 14
    early technology 87, 88
sports, clothing for 92
spreadsheets 43
stain-resistant finishes 28
staple fibres 10, 11
stencils 24
storyboards 69, 70
straightstitched hem 52
subsystems 74
surface decoration 25–7
surface finishes 28–9

sweatshirt, design 67
synthetic fibres 7–8, 14
systems 72–3

taped seam 50
technical textiles 91, 94
Tencel 93
tents 29, 92
testing
    fabrics 31–4
    product 69ñ70
textiles 1
      uses 2, 91–2, 94
texture 60
tiedyeing 23
toile 77
tone (colour) 60
tools and equipment 46–9
Trade Descriptions Act 37, 84
Trading Standards Officers 37, 84
transfers 25
tweed 16
twill weave 15

uniforms 91

Velcro 55
VileneÆ 18
viscose 7

wad 12
wadding 18, 22
waistcoat, production 43, 75–9
warp knitting 18
water-repellent finishes 28
waxing 28
weaving 14, 87–8
weft knitting 17
wool 5, 10, 11, 12
    blends 11
woollen yarns 10, 13
working drawings 68
workwear 91
worsted 10, 13
woven fabrics 14–16

yarn 1

zips 53–4